Enigmas
medieval

Contents

Elixir

Yesterday, Nicolas Flamel went and bought a bottle of elixir of quintessence for his experiments in alchemy. He paid 30 crowns and we know that the elixir was worth 29 crowns more than the little vial.

Can you, cunning reader, say how much he paid for the pretty vial?

Solution p. 155.

The Damsel of the Short Sleeves

'But Sire, my heart beats only for him, he is my hero, my sun, my sweetmeat. In short, I love him …' begged the Damsel of the Short Sleeves.

'It's just not going to be possible!' ruled Arthur, kindly but very firmly.

'But why, Sire?'

'Come now, Damsel of the Short Sleeves, is it not the case that you are also called the Ugly Damsel? Do I have to draw you a picture?'

'But do you not believe, Sire, that ugliness is in the eye of the beholder?'

Keep going, this is fascinating stuff. thought the king.

'And is not beauty of the soul the greatest beauty of all?'

Lucky I'm sitting down. thought the king.

'Was Socrates beautiful? Or Aesop, with his hunch?'

Here we go, I'm going to get a philosophy lesson now.

'In short, appearances are often misleading. For example myself, who is speaking to you and needs your help: do you know that there is a place I can sit where, though you are king you cannot?'

The king went from irritation to pity and, looking over the ugly Damsel – who could easily have been called the Damsel of the Short Thighs as the Damsel of the Short Sleeves – he finally said, hardly imagining that she could perch herself on any inaccessible heights:

'If what you say is true, Damsel, I will put your case to the knight of your heart's desire … Otherwise, I will not put up with you bothering me any more. Is that clear?'

'Crystal, Sire' she replied, her frog-like face twisting into a wicked smirk of satisfaction.

Why?

Solution p. 157.

Merry-go-round

An endless, plaintive cry rose up from Brother Gastule: 'A horse for each, a horse for each, and good ones too! All different, what's more! Whims, demands! Not one who likes the same colour coat as the others! And a horse dealer who can only offer me a bay horse, a dappled horse, a piebald horse, a chestnut horse and a buckskin horse!'

It's true he had a difficult task: Arthur swore by bay horses alone, Perceval and Gawain despised buckskin horses, Perceval and Lancelot had eyes only for chestnuts, which the others shunned completely; Galahad wouldn't hear of either chestnut or dappled horses.

Once calm is restored beneath Brother Gastule's cowl and he stops moaning and feeling sorry for himself enough to think for a bit, which horse will he give to each?

Solution p. 157.

The game of chess

On Saturdays, the knights Galahad and Perceval play chess, which is to say, the pre-modern game and not yet what came to be called 'Mad Queen's Chess': on a board with red and white squares, the Queen can only move one square, diagonally — any Guinevere knows that her powers are limited, that it will be some time before Cosette has the right to vote. But if the games are slower, they are no less fiercely contested …

This particular Saturday, however, Sir Galahad and Sir Perceval played seven games — that's right, seven.

The chronicle tells us that each won as many games as the other. And yet, it's not that there were any stalemates: no drawn games in sight.

Should we say, reader, that the chronicle lies?

Solution p. 158.

Name skeletons

During a memorable battle of the Hundred Years War, the soldiers lost the vowels from their first names.

Are you able to complete these name skeletons?

A warning: their name may have begun with a vowel …

Solution p. 148.

NGRRAD

JHN

CLTR

GVN

The big barter

Jehanne adores eggs. She goes to the market. But at this market, everything is bartered and swapped and nothing is bought! She has two pumpkins — how can she get a dozen eggs?

On the first stall, a sign reads:
'Here we exchange a bunch of leeks and a marrow for a dozen eggs'.

On the second stall, a sign reads:
'Here we exchange a pumpkin for two quails'.

On the third stall, a sign reads:
'Here we exchange a pumpkin for a marrow'.

On the fourth stall, a sign reads:
'Here we exchange two quails for a bunch of leeks'.

Solution p. 156.

9

Arithmetic

Jacquemin and Isembert are trying to steal a jar of redcurrant jam placed on a shelf so high that neither of them can reach it. One will have to get up on the shoulders of the other. The first of them is 1.2 metres tall and the second 1.4 metres.

Which of the two should get up on the shoulders of the other to have the most chance of reaching the shelf: Jacquemin or Isembert?

Solution p. 124.

The Flush

Queen Guinevere has dropped the silver-gilt and pearl-encrusted comb, which the king brought back for her from Mont Saint-Michel, into the moat from the top of the tower, *plop*! Lancelot has done his best playing the frogman, but he isn't able to find it. The queen at her window howls, whimpers, snivels and stamps her feet. Desperate times call for desperate measures, says her gallant escort — the most radical solution is to drain the moat.

The operation can be carried out using three pipes, usually hermetically sealed, accessible via a foul-smelling underground passage and through which the water can be dumped into a bottomless pit, just below that small room behind a yellow door at the end of the corridor on the left, called the garderobe or comfort station. One of these pipes can drain the whole moat in 8 days, the second takes 12 days, and 24 days are needed for the third one to do its job.

If Lancelot activates all three pipes at once, how many days will it be before the queen stops whining?

Solution p. 158.

Smooth operator

— Stop right there, knight, answer my question and I'll let you pass. And if I'm not satisfied with your response, you and your horse will be but a mouthful for my dragon.
Barbequiou, lie down!

Here is my riddle:

My keys have no locks

Anyone can come caress me

From top to bottom — I never tire

Just murmur and whisper

What on earth is it?

Solution p. 155.

One for three, three for eight

Galahad, Ywain and Perceval each considered in turn the thin and quite round fouace loaf that the Red Knight pointed out to them and the eight sinister-looking creatures sitting in a row at the great table of the convent — a convent that, by the looks of things, is haunted.

'These here are the Devil's creatures, My Lords, and none has yet done battle with them without leaving behind a piece of their anatomy, which has been used to feed the hellhounds — can you hear them growling behind the thick walls? But this whole fine company will leave you in peace if you deign to serve my guests this modest fouace. A warning, nonetheless: you have to give them equal portions and each of you is only allowed to use your own sword, once only.'

'Let's turn round and go back, I have no desire for my leg to end up in a mongrel's stomach' says Ywain.

'If we have to perform magic tricks, we should have brought Merlin with us' sighed Galahad.

'What a load of carry-on!' Perceval exclaimed, grabbing his sword. 'It's the work of a minute!'

How?

Solution p. 159.

Oh how many unicorns, how many melusines ...

Galahad and Bors were going back to Camelot, and along the way they compared notes on their recollections to save time when they had to submit reports to Father Blaise, so he could keep a record of their exploits for posterity.

In particular they had gone into a chapel where the walls boasted a collection of perfectly frightful stuffed animals, an extraordinary group of monsters.

There were, they remembered, Unicorns, which are beasts with a single horn; Pirassoipis, unicorns from Arabia with two horns, and Melusines, who are both serpent and woman and have no horns at all. They could still see in their mind's eye the 28 glass eyes staring down on them.

'I remember' said Galahad, 'counting 15 horns!'
'I remember' said Bors, 'adding up 36 feet!'
'Well then,' said Brother Gastule, who was following them on an old mule, 'in that case you can tell Father Blaise how many Melusines, Unicorns and Pirassoipis there were!'

How many, then?

Solution p. 159.

Graeco-Latin square

Remember that a magic square is an ancestor of sudoku: in a
4 x 4 grid we have 4 numbers, but each occurs only once in
each row, each column and each diagonal.
This Graeco-Latin square is made up of two magic squares
combined together and 'superimposed' on each other. You have
to separate them to work out the two original grids.

*Clue: the bigger
numbers stay
together.*

Solution p. 130.

CI	XV	XXII	LIII
XXIII	LII	CV	XI
LV	XXI	XIII	CII
XII	CIII	LI	XXV

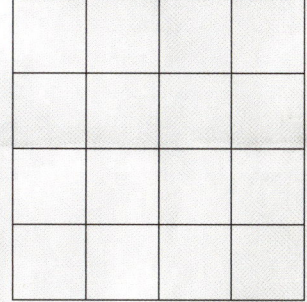

Thanking the squire

Arthur has to leave the castle of Camelot and head to Ireland to negotiate an important treaty aimed at protecting the export of soft fermented cheeses. As he has five solid hours of horseback riding to reach the sea, he asks the squire who has the job of keeping watch near his royal bedchamber to wake him up at 3 o'clock in the morning, on the dot.

At the designated hour the squire knocks on the door, enters and immediately begs the king to stay at Camelot. 'The Lady of the Lake, Sire, appeared to me in a dream to tell me that your ship will be the victim of unfortunate circumstances at sea which will capsize it, and all shall perish — passengers and cargo, women, children and soft fermented cheese samples.'
'Hm!' thinks Arthur. 'If the Lady of the Lake is getting mixed up in the affair and taking it upon herself to appear to simpletons, it must be serious. Too bad, then, I'll stay!'

A wise decision! Because two days later he learns from a reliable source that the boat he was going to take caught in a storm that whipped up waves as high as his castle's dungeon; it sank and all the passengers drowned.
He had the man who saved his life brought to him, and said to him: 'Thank you! Really, I must sincerely express my gratitude to you. Also, you're fired!'

Why?

Solution p. 160.

Pigments

Last week Nicolas Flamel bought himself some coloured pigments for his experiments in alchemy. Two small labels were attached to each small bag. But he is clumsy and they've all come off.

Can you help him work out the names of the different pigments?

Solution p. 128.

He has on the one hand:	And on the other:
Yellow	Saint John's
Green	German
Black	Rouen
Red	Egyptian
Blue	Naples
White	Brazilian

A few clues to help you: the blue isn't European, the black isn't associated with a town, the red has a third of the number of letters of its pair, and the white is as pure in name as in nature, so to speak.

Forest of figures

Lusignan Forest is a muddle of paths. To get their bearings, the woodcutters have made a map, but not so simple that any poachers who found it could easily use it.

They therefore noted down on the map the number of paths that leave in different directions from particular points.

All you have to do is draw the paths that join the Roman numerals together, using this clue, in order to draw the map of this section of the forest.

Solution p. 129.

Jeu de mérelle

The 'jeu de mérelle' is a very old board game from the Middle Ages. Each player has ten pieces: one has white pieces, the other has black pieces. The winner is the first one to make a line of pieces in his own colour following the straight lines of the game board.

We are in the middle of a match between two squires, who each have two pieces to play. It's Eudes's turn to play. He's using the white pieces: where should he place his piece to be sure of winning?

Solution p. 134.

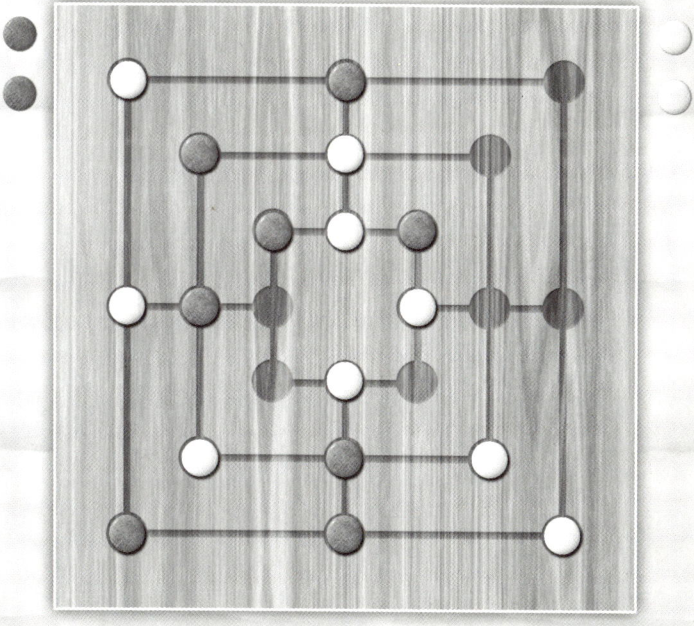

Sunday's child

In the Castle of Pesme Aventure there is, inside a large enclosure surrounded by stakes, a workshop where seven times 52 young Ottoman women in rags make pieces in gold and silk. The knight Ywain considers these young girls seated on thirty benches opposite him with both indignation and pity: quite clearly he has just stumbled across a secret 'sweatshop'.

At the same time as he goes over Article L 324 of the Work Code in his head, Ywain wonders what the odds are that the young lady seated at the far left of the seventh bench was born on a Sunday.

Solution p. 156.

At home or on the town?

The wife of a rich and widowed vavasour had her life perfectly ordered. Monday, she went to visit the poor of her parish. She spent her Tuesdays in the castle kitchen, going over things with her cook and housekeeper. Wednesday was devoted to music, and she kept to a small salon where she took lessons from one minstrel or another. There was no Thursday that she did not dedicate to her elderly mother, who lived in a small country house just by the church. Friday was housework day; she supervised the chambermaids and wasn't too proud to pick up a feather duster herself. Saturday, rain or wind, she accompanied the vavasour on a long horse ride. Sunday, she stayed in her room and did strictly nothing.

Next Christmas, which will be a Wednesday, where will she be?

Solution p.160.

Featherweight

One of Brother Gastule's duties at Camelot is to look after the feeding of the birds that the queen keeps locked up for her pleasure in a beautiful golden cage. It's not a very difficult task: it has been agreed that the monk has to give the birds the equivalent of their weight, and he takes care every morning to pour 45 ounces of millet into the feeder.

But come springtime the birds are tearing out each other's feathers instead of singing, and Guinevere decides that from now on they'll be kept in separate cages.

If the jay weighs a quarter of the total weight of the two other birds, and the heaviest bird, a budgerigar, weighs 3 ounces less than the two others combined, how will our good Brother distribute the daily millet from now on?

Solution p. 160.

Carousel

Two white Knights and two black Knights have been placed at the four corners of a nine-square chessboard.
Let's remind ourselves how a Knight moves in chess:

Following these rules, can you place the white Knights on the left and the black Knights on the right onto the same squares?
Solution p. 132.

The Aymon boys' nags

Duke Aymon's four sons were all born on Christmas Day, and are all different ages. On their birthday, between the turkey and Mass, their father gives them wooden horses, nasty little nags in red-lead painted boxwood. He gives each of them as many horses as they are years old.

On that particular Christmas, Richardet, the youngest, counted the horses that were meant for them waiting beneath the chimney, and says that there are exactly three times more than five years before.

How old is the oldest son?

Solution p. 161.

Just a question of time

For this kind of thing, it was best not to rely too much on Brother Gastule … Thus it was the wizard Merlin whom Mordred, son of Arthur, approached with his strange request: 'Give me, I beg you, a potion to go back in time 60 years.'

'Not a problem, my boy, it's just a question of time!' replied Merlin.

Three moons afterwards, in effect, Merlin gave him a bitter — oh how bitter! — concoction to drink under the great oak tree, which dispatched him straightaway, for just one hour, to a time when his grandfather Uther Pendragon was playing marbles in short hose with his brothers Constans and Ambrosius Aurelianus. Ah! Dirty, disgraceful Pendragon, the shame of the family, at this age the thought had not yet occurred to him to make the king of Cornwall a cuckold by insinuating himself under false pretences into the bed of the beautiful Ygraine! And in a fit of retrospective rage Mordred unsheathed his sword, rushed at him and killed him.

Two hours later, beneath the great oak tree, Mordred had still not come back.

Why, Merlin wondered, would that be?

Solution p. 162.

The minstrel

A minstrel has the job of writing a song to the glory of
Charlemagne. But he no longer has a very clear memory of
the episodes of his reign.
Help him put the events of Charlemagne's life back in
chronological order. In so doing, the town in which he died
will appear.

**A. Charlemagne reigns alone over the
kingdom of the Franks.**

E. Submission of the Saxons.

A. Victory in Aquitaine.

H. Charlemagne crowned Holy Emperor.

N. Canonisation.

C. Submission of the Lombards.

Solution p. 138.

Name skeletons

During a memorable battle of the Hundred Years War, the soldiers lost the vowels from their first names.

Are you able to complete these name skeletons?

A warning: their name may have begun with a vowel ...

Solution p. 148.

BRTHLM

NSTR

RLND

TNG

Puzzle

Can you reconstruct this town landscape?

Place the pieces A, B, C, D, E and F into the squares numbered 1 to 6.

Solution p. 141.

A

B

C

D

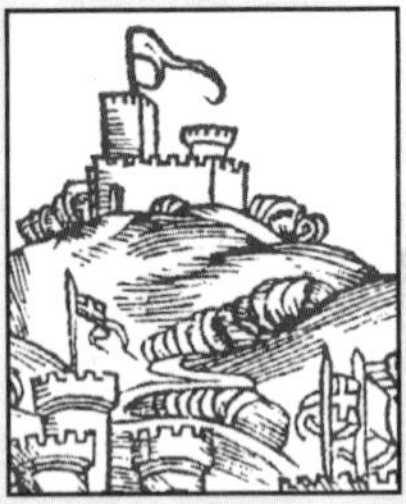

E

F

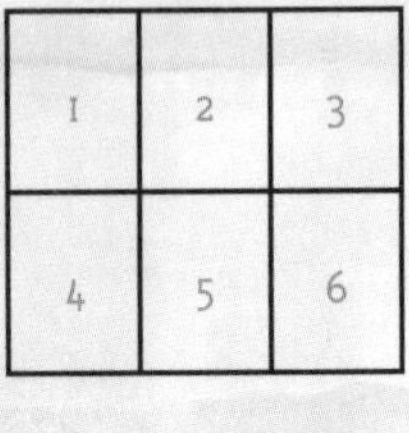

I	2	3
4	5	6

Who does what?

Three monks — Brother John, Brother William and Brother François — have found a small chest by the wayside. Before taking it to the convent superior, they would like to open it to see what's inside. But obviously they don't have the key!
Each of the three will try to open it, one way or another.

One tries to insert the point of a knife into the keyhole. The second tugs on it with his teeth. The third takes a rock and gives the opening a violent blow, all without the least success.

Result: a crushed thumb, a cut forefinger and a broken tooth!

Who does what with what, if:
 • **Brother John has no knife;**
 • **Brother William doesn't injure his fingers.**

Fill out the table below

Name	Instrument	Result

Solution p. 146.

The perilous bridge

About to enter the Kingdom of Gorre, where Queen Guinevere is being kept prisoner, Lancelot beholds, at the turn of the path, an abyss of the murkiest kind opening up beneath his feet. He sees, wide-eyed, two sinister vultures circling beneath him, and he can just glimpse the whitened bones of a horse's skeleton way down below. What's more, it's raining.

There are two bridges before him, one guarded by a red knight who's all dressed in red, from his stirrups to his crest, the other by a black knight, black from head to toe, from the feathers on his helmet to the sollerets on his feet. Suddenly a page appears, wearing quartered hose, half-black, half-red, who says more or less the following:
'Hello there, my Lord knight, one of these bridges will let you cross over the border safe and sound and enter the kingdom of Gorre — at your own risk, of course. The other will give way beneath your feet halfway across and plunge you into the abyss, and what's more, it's raining. To help you in your decision, you can ask one question, and one question only to one — and only one — of the two guardians of these two bridges. Be aware, Sire, however, that while one of them always tells the truth, the other lies all the time.'

'Thank you very much for the tip, Page,' Lancelot replied, moving forward confidently, 'it will be of great use to me ...'

And if you yourself were a valiant knight, what question would you ask to be sure of getting across the abyss?

Solution p. 163.

The map is not the territory

Gawain, the flower of chivalry, is desperately seeking his beloved
Lunete. Lunete, accused of treason by Lady Laudine's seneschal,
and threatened with being burned alive, is in great need of a
champion to defend her honour. But even when you're the flower
of chivalry, when you're face to face with a giant who's two toises
high, screaming into your ears, map in hand, that Lunete is on
HIS territory and that whomever wants to enter HIS territory has to
challenge him personally, you think twice …

'Very well!' Gawain finally declares, taking his fingers out of his
ears, 'Very well then! I challenge you to … to put your hands into
your pockets and put both feet on either side of this meandering
blue line that runs across the parchment of your map, right down
the middle, and which represents, I imagine, the Escarpolette
river. For if you cannot, you should indeed consider, Sire, that God
doesn't wish you to claim absolute possession of your territory.'

'And you're planning, I suppose, to turn the parchment over, or
hang it on the wall, or tear it up, or eat it raw with a small dish of
sea salt?'

'I shall not, Sire, I shall place it on the ground and not touch it
again, unless to place your feet upon it.'

'It's a deal!' says the giant, though not before comparing the size
of his shoes and that of the parchment.

You're trapped like the big fat rat that you are … thought Gawain.

What does Gawain, the flower of chivalry, do?

Solution p. 164.

Fiddling the figures

Let's remind ourselves of the Roman numerals:

1	5	10	50	100	500	1000
I	V	X	L	C	D	M

If you write the number 1968 in Roman numerals, and then take just one of each Roman numeral used, what new number do you get?

Solution p. 154.

Baring the teeth

Deep inside the cave, eight small bags on a low table, a dwarf in green hose and some scales. Fifteen feet from the bags are Lancelot and Galahad, armed to the teeth and ready to pounce. But between the bags and the knights are solid bronze bars and a ditch filled to the brim with horned vipers. And just for good measure, between the grill and the ditch, three lions wandering back and forth who for the last fifteen days have been fed on good high-fibre, bowel-cleansing brown rice.

'Come on, give us the bag of dragon teeth your master promised the wizard Merlin, so we can get out of here quick smart!'

'They're not just any dragon teeth, they're dragon incisors. And, you're going to laugh, but my master forgot to tell me which bag it was … the other seven contain cocodrile incisors.'

'So open them up, you green-hosed dunderhead! Surely you'll recognise them!'

'You are rather ready, Sire, to bare your own teeth … The dunderhead is pleased to inform you that nothing resembles a dragon incisor more than a cocodrile incisor. The only difference is their weight: the cocodrile incisor weighs 10 grains, and the dragon's twice as much, it's in a different category when it comes to quality. I'm happy to do a weighing for Merlin's sake; but since I am a dunderhead, I will do one, and one only.'

'Obviously weighing a bag at random doesn't get us anywhere … A vile pestilence on the pen-pushing hack who put his hand to enigma-writing and who's done his best to put us in a situation that prevents us from touching the bags in question with either our hands or our feet!' grumbled Galahad.

'Stop your sulking, I've got the solution.'

How will Lancelot solve the problem?

Solution p. 164.

Knight in green sauce

To avenge the honour of Gawain, Ywain (the Knight of the Lion)
has just finished off the Green Knight fair and square in his
Hautdesert castle. The latter made it about 30 metres trying to
save his own skin but ended up slipping on the parquetry floor.
Now that he's lying there on the ground in a pool of greenish
blood, still twitching a little and his eyes rolling furiously, Ywain
remembers that when Gawain decapitated him on a previous
occasion, the Green Knight had left, whistling, his head under his
arm, like it was something that happened every day.

'This time, old chum, you won't even have time to count your
fingers and toes, and I won't give you the chance to come back!'
mutters Ywain. He whistles to his lion and invites him to the
picnic, asking him to hurry up because he should go quickly to
tell the good news to knight Louya.

And since it generally takes his pet no less than twelve hours to
devour a green knight, Ywain opens the window to let in the wolf,
who can get down two-thirds of a green knight in a day, and the
vultures, much less productive, who need four days. And since
it's a celebratory feast and he is very fond of animals, he calls
on a band of maggots of his acquaintance to help, particularly
voracious maggots who can do the same thing in twelve days.

**If all of Ywain's friends get straight down to work, how long it
will it take before we can play knucklebones?**

Solution p. 165.

The accursed number

Have you ever had a nightmare more terrifying than the one that woke Lancelot in a start, who had simply dozed off beneath a large acorn tree in Brocéliande forest: "No! Not seventeen! For pity's sake, not the number seventeen!" he cried out, sweating and gasping for breath as if the devil in person had appeared to him.

So why the fearful panic?

Solution p. 165.

Aucassin and Nicole

Aucassin and Nicole are very much in love and are therefore inseparable. Wherever Aucassin is, Nicole is by his side. Each Aucassin ✖ thus has beside him a Nicole ▼.

The rules:
The figures above the columns and in front of the rows indicate the number of times Nicole ▼ appears there. Find the 18 Nicoles hidden in the grid, if:

• There are as many Aucassins ✖ as Nicoles ▼.
• Each square containing a ▼ must be paired, on one of its sides, by a square containing a ✖.
• Two squares containing a ▼ can't touch each other either by the sides or the corners.

Solution p. 125.

	2	2	3	1	3	2	3	2
3		✖						✖
1		✖			✖	✖		✖
3		✖						
0								
3	✖			✖		✖		
0								
3	✖		✖		✖			
1								
1		✖	✖		✖			✖
3						✖		

Apocalypse now

Morholt arrived at a town traversed by a river and girded by a triple ring of ramparts, and all the horses in his army reared up at the drum-rolls issuing from the battlements.
Heralds appeared, trumpets in hand.

The first trumpet brought forth from the North Gate a black knight who had killed a fifth of Morholt's army.
At the second trumpet a red knight appeared from the South Gate, and hurled an eighth of them into the flames.
At the third trumpet, a green knight, bursting out of the West Gate, threw a twelfth of them into the river.
At the sound of the fourth, a white knight opened the gate on the side of the rising sun and carried off a quarter.
The fifth trumpet was the signal to cut the throats of a twentieth of the army.
The sixth unleashed wrath on a seventh of Morholt's troops.
The seventh hadn't finished ringing out when 220 of Morholt's cavalrymen disappeared, silently swallowed up by a sudden gulf that opened up beneath their horses' steps. Twelve died stricken with terror, 3 others from appalling diarrhoea, and 15, disregarding all thoughts of honour, deserted in quite a hurry.

Morholt came back with an army of 20 men.

How many men were under his command in the beginning?

Solution p. 166.

Knights in search of a title

Three wandering knights are travelling incognito and in convoy, meaning they are travelling together and that, against all custom, they are wearing a plain coat of armour and not bearing any coat of arms or motto. All that we can see is that one is wearing a green plume on top of his helmet, and the other two a red and a black plume, respectively.

The contingencies of their trip have meant that riding pillion with them are a countess, a duchess and a baroness. An amazing coincidence: one of the knights is a count, another a duke and the third a baron, but we don't know who is carrying whom.

We do know this, however:
1. The countess resides in the castle of the king of Cambremer.
2. The black knight lives in the royal castle of the kingdom of Orkney.
3. The duchess doesn't know how to play chess.
4. The fair lady who bears the same title as the black knight lives in the castle of Camelot.
5. The black knight and the fair lady who knows how to play chess share the privilege of attending the queen's supper.
6. The baron organises falconry parties with the green knight.

What title does the red knight bear?

Solution p. 167.

Forest of Figures

Lusignan Forest is a muddle of paths. To get their bearings, the woodcutters have made a map, but not so simple that any poachers who found it could easily use it.

They therefore noted down on the map the number of paths that leave in different directions from particular points.

All you have to do is draw the paths that join the Roman numerals together, using this clue, in order to draw the map of this section of the forest. *Solution p. 132.*

I II   II I

III II III II

II III II II

II III   II

II III   II

The value of things

Every day Merlin and Barnabas go to the mill to grind their wheat and receive a bag of flour each.

If I tell you that Merlin has already received 30 bags of flour and Barnabas 9, can you tell me how many days it will take for Merlin to have received exactly twice as many bags of four as Barnabas? *Solution p. 137.*

The drakkars

You have to work out the position of the Norman drakkars using the coordinate grid on the opposite page. The figures indicate the number of squares in the row or column occupied by a ship. Watch out! Each boat is surrounded by water (two boats can't touch each other). To help you, we have identified a few empty squares. The reefs prevent anyone from navigating through there.

Solution p. 139.

You have to find:

▢▢▢▢ 3 long drakkars
▢▢▢ 4 skeiðs
▢▢ 4 snekkjas
▢ 3 longboats

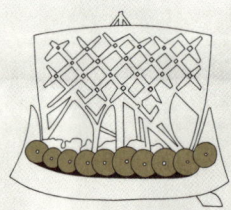

	4	1	4	3	5	2	4	4	3	2	3	
												4
												1
												2
												6
												1
												0
												3
												6
												1
												2
												1
												7
												1

The legacy of the vavasour

The dream had begun rather pleasantly. It presented the valiant knights Bors, Galahad and Perceval, to whom a grateful vavasour had left the horses in his stables. The vavasour's widow, while leading them to the building, explained a restrictive clause in this provision of the will: half the horses were to go to Bors, a third to Galahad, and Perceval, who was only half listening, was to receive one-ninth of the legacy.

The dream turned into a nightmare when out of the stables came ... seventeen horses. 'Right then!' shouted Perceval, brandishing his longsword in both hands. 'We just have to neatly cut that one in two! Bors, you'll be able to leave with your eight and a half horses and as for me I'm going to fix myself a pot-au-feu and eat it on the spot, someone peel me a few turnips!' In his dream, Lancelot arrived right at that moment and his proud battle steed, who had no love for turnips, reared up. Thus it was that he woke up screaming: 'Not seventeen! Sweet merciful God, not the number seventeen!'

'What an idiot I am,' he said, pulling himself together. 'I had the solution to the problem right there ...'

Do you, like Lancelot, know how to solve the problem so as to avoid bloodshed, while still observing the rules of the division?

Solution p. 167.

Jeu de mérelle

The 'jeu de mérelle' is a very old board game from the Middle Ages. Each player has 10 pieces: one has white pieces, the other has black pieces. The winner is the first one to make a line of three pieces in his own colour following the straight lines of the game board.

We are in the middle of a match between two squires, who each have a few pieces left to play. It's Eudes's turn, he's using the black pieces: where should he place his piece to be sure of winning?

Solution p. 135.

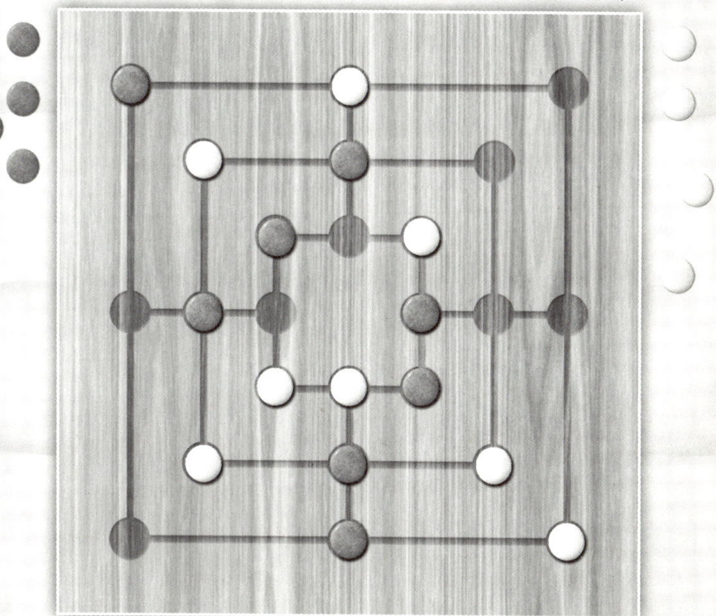

Up to here

'So is that posson of mead coming? The braised peacock can hardly wait forever, little monk!'

'Is this cook kidding?' grumbled Brother Gastule, cramped under his monk's cowl. 'A posson, a posson, how does he expect me to pull a posson from this blasted barrel of mead when there's only two containers in this kitchen, one that holds a chopine and the other a demiard! No, really, I've had it up to here!'

Understand, modern reader, that at the court of Camelot a chopine was the equivalent of half of one of your litres, a demiard 300 millilitres, and a posson, as called for by the chef to blend with some verjuice for his sauce, an even 100 millilitres.

Will you be a more adroit kitchenhand than Brother Gastule? Will Arthur get his sweet-and-sour peacock?

Solution p. 168.

Puzzle

Can you reconstruct this town landscape?

Place the pieces A, B, C, D, E and F into the squares numbered 1 to 6.

Solution p. 142.

A

B

C

D

E

F

1	2	3
4	5	6

Token collection

Eduald collects numbered tokens and as he has a passion for logic, he doesn't want to present his collection in any ordinary way. He has a small tray made for himself on which he can arrange his tokens in a very cunning way — in fact, without realising it, he has invented sudoku! The filling of the tray is subject to the same constraints: each number appears only once in each row, each column and in each of the 9 groups of 3x3 squares.

But Eduald has just knocked over the tray! Fortunately, to help him remember how the tokens were arranged, Eduald has marked numbers around the grid representing the sum of the numbers up to the first thicker line (towards the left, right, up or down). Can you help him put his collection back?

Solution p. 149.

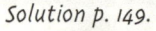

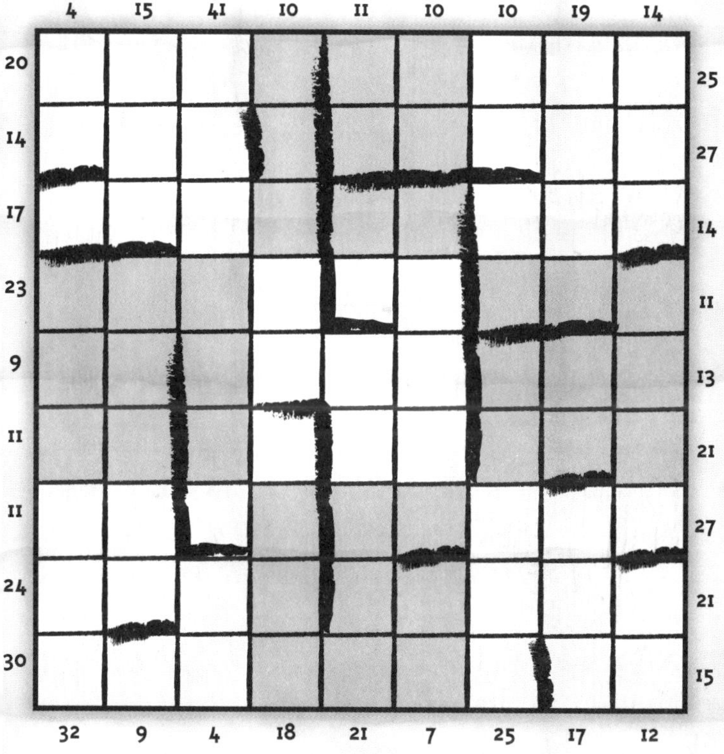

	4	15	41	10	11	10	10	19	14	
20										25
14										27
17										14
23										11
9										13
11										21
11										27
24										21
30										15
	32	9	4	18	21	7	25	17	12	

47

Who does what?

Coming back from three markets — Lombardy market, Saint-Barnabé market and Saint-Omer market — three brothers, Clodomir, Berenger and Angelin, are telling each other the stories of their ups and downs. They each have a different trade: furrier, draper and dairyman. Now Angelin speaks:

'I'm really happy: once again I've managed to sell all my milk at the market. As for you, Berenger, they'll never be able to shift you from Lombardy, and I understand that you, Clodomir, are congratulating yourself that you didn't go to Saint-Barnabé, where the draper's corner is right next to the foul-smelling furriers.'

Complete the table below:

Name	Trade	Place
Angelin		
Berenger		
Clodomir		

Solution p. 147.

Name skeletons

During a memorable battle of the Hundred Years War, the soldiers lost the vowels from their first names.
Are you able to complete these name skeletons?

A warning: their name may have begun with a vowel …

CHLDBRT

DGBRT

CLVS

GNHRD

Solution p. 148.

At Wastefoolnesse Castle

At Wastefoolnesse Castle the glasses have holes in them, they throw their écus out the window and they fritter away their time — indeed, they have nothing for measuring time. Which is extremely unfortunate for Brother Gastule, who has a cauldron of potion going on the stove which has to stay on a rolling boil for exactly one hour and 45 minutes, goodness gracious it's vexing.

The only thing that can give an idea of how much time is passing is a small candelabra with six branches, each of which is topped by a small cup with a spike in the middle. On the six spikes six small candles are stuck, and the amount of wax is such that the life of each of the small candles is one hour.

It's not possible, however, to measure half an hour by cutting a candle in half, because the base is much thicker than the top, and the lower the flame gets, the slower the wax melts.

All that Brother Gastule has at his disposal is the small candelabra with the six small candles, a penknife, a hammer, an anvil and three clothes pegs. What will he do?

Solution p. 168.

The guillotine doors

'Curses!' grumbles Ywain.

Just after he crossed the drawbridge of Esclados-the-Red's castle in close pursuit of his enemy, a guillotine door abruptly dropped down in front of him and obliged him to pull up short, while behind him another one, falling right behind his spurred heels, has just cut his horse in half.

Fortunately, through a narrow opening in the castle's fortifications he can just glimpse a damsel, who offers to help him.

Unfortunately, he's going to have to think sitting on half a horse, bathing in a pool of blood and guts.

Fortunately, as a general rule, a horse is only very moderately useful for solving enigmas of this kind as given by the damsel:

'On your left, knight, you will see four rings. You can engage the mechanism that raises the guillotine doors by giving them the number of complete turns that I'm going to indicate. I suggest you take notes:

— the total number of complete turns is 13;

— the number of turns of the third ring is equal to the sum of the turns that you will have performed on the first two rings;

— if you add the number of turns of the first ring and the number of turns of the last ring, you get 9 turns.

Ah! I almost forgot: you have to give each of the rings a different number of turns …'

With or without your favourite horse can you, reader, work out the rescuing combination?

Solution p. 169.

Arithmetic

Brother John is an excellent calligrapher but he's also a good mathematician. So he likes to set out mathematical operations and try to solve them. This time he has set out the following operation, in which the different letters correspond to different values:

$$
\begin{array}{rccc}
 & B & & A \\
 & C & & B \\
+ & C & VIII & C \\
\hline
 & A & A & A \\
\end{array}
$$

And he wonders what the value of A must be for this operation to be correct.

Solution p. 124.

No Bénédictine in the goblette

After numerous adventures the valiant Bors is getting ready to leave the sinister realm of Gorre, but not without taking with him some clear evidence of his feats: a dragon whose legs he has shackled and wings he has clipped and a horrid goblin of the female sex — a goblette, if you will — with skin of a greenish hue and a very black soul, both of whom had caused endless torment to a nice man, a wise and pious hermit.

As an expression of his gratitude the hermit, as a wise and pious man, offered Bors a small barrel of fermented liquid, or about 130 litres of a home brew that could, at a stretch, pass for Bénédictine on the occasion, for example, of a joyful and drunken reunion around a Round Table.

The problem that Bors faces is as follows: to leave the kingdom of Gorre he has to cross the river, and the boat available to him for this purpose is so small that he can only take one of his three belongings on the crossing: either the goblin, the dragon or the barrel.

The goblin, however, is a veritable sponge in female form who has but one desire, which is to partake of the contents of the barrel. The dragon, for his part, runs on mineral water, but isn't above a tasty hors d'oeuvre and he could make short work of some goblin carpaccio.

Dear me, my good damsel, nothing is simple and it's all getting rather complicated.

How will Bors bring back all three?   *Solution p. 169.*

Abacus

This is an abacus reset to zero. To represent a number, you move the beads towards the centre beam. Only the beads next to the centre beam are counted.

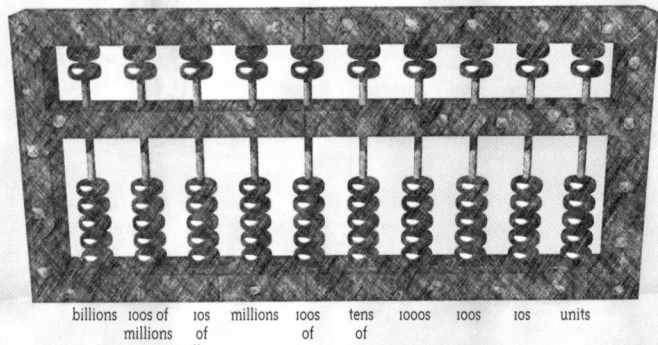

= 5

= 1

billions	100s of millions	10s of millions	millions	100s of 1000s	tens of 1000s	1000s	100s	10s	units

So, what number is represented on the abacus below?

Solution p. 127.

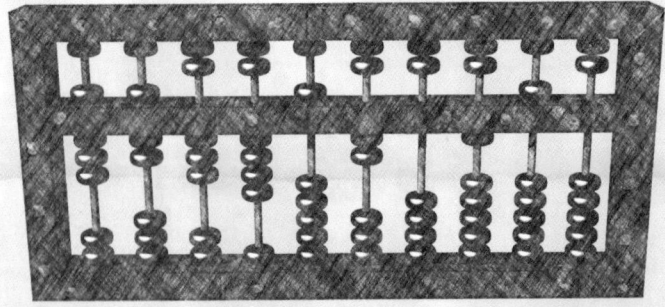

54

Graeco-Latin square

Remember that a magic square is an ancestor of sudoku: there are 4 numbers in a 4 × 4 grid, but each occurs only once in each row, each column and each diagonal.

This Graeco-Latin square is made up of two magic squares combined together and 'superimposed' on each other. You have to separate them to work out the two original grids.

Clue:
single numerals
stick together.

Solution p. 130.

CCL	XII	XXI	MMC
CXX	MMI	CCX	LII
MMX	LXX	CII	CCI
III	CCC	MML	XXX

The Bridge of Mists

They were four well-battered knights with an inconvenient giant hot on their heels: an indistinct sort of creature that the peasants called Zieu, a sort of formless, foul-smelling and evil-doing mass, a real pile of mud. Lancelot had a knee the size of a watermelon, Bors was limping, Perceval was dragging his left leg behind him and Gawain was practically crawling. They only had a 30-minute lead on their new playmate, and a terrible abyss had just opened up in front of them, around a sharp bend, something like a deadend. What's more, the weather was rainy and there was a fog you could cut with a broadsword.

Just as Gawain was about to say that their turnips were well and truly cooked, Lancelot noticed a sign on which was written, in pen and ink in an uncial script, 'Bridge of Mists: two people at a time max.' Perceval asked if anyone had heard of this Max, and Bors started railing against Seneschal Kay and all his kind, no doubt confusing the seneschal's office and the department of bridges and roads, because no bridge was there to be seen.

At that point, amidst the prevailing idiocy, Lancelot remembered that the Lady of the Lake had once, long ago in the palace of Avalon, given him a magic necklace that clears fog — now there's a stroke of luck. And, in effect, he only had to rub the medallion that hung on the chain for a bridge to appear, materialising in the shape of an arc between the two vertical rock faces of the abyss. He handed the necklace to Perceval, who wanted to see the miracle up close: the bridge disappeared. Perceval rubbed the medallion in turn: the bridge reappeared.

'When Perceval has finished playing, we'll need to get a move on!' said Lancelot, to urge on his wounded troops. While he himself with his busted knee could cover the distance in 3 minutes, the limper would need 4, it would take 8 minutes for the one with the gammy leg, and as for Gawain, he would need 12 minutes.

Given all of that, and taking into account the fact that they had already lost 2 minutes, would they all have time to get across, using the necklace, before Zieu the giant came along to make inquiries as to their health?

Solution p. 170.

I is for isosceles

'Too easy!' said Brother Gastule under his breath.

He had closed the old and venerable manuscript Bible he was asked to copy out, and in its place had put on the lectern a fragment of parchment that he had found between two psalms. While he hummed 'The Lord is my Shepherd' in Latin to the tune of *La Paimpolaise*, Brother Gastule recognised an isosceles triangle in the drawing of three equal lines joined together, which allowed him to decipher without too much difficulty most of the words that a faint and clumsy hand had traced inside the triangle in question:

'There are ... examples of the letter i in this isosceles triangle.'

There was just the word between 'are' and 'examples', which time had erased, to fill in. Too easy?

Solution p. 171.

Forest of figures

Lusignan Forest is a muddle of paths. To get their bearings,
the woodcutters have made a map, but not so simple that any
poachers who found it could easily use it.

They therefore noted down on the map the number of paths that
leave in different directions from particular points.

All you have to do is draw the paths that join the Roman numerals
together, using this clue, in order to draw the map of this section
of the forest.

Solution p. 133.

III		II		II	
	II		II		
IV	II	I	III	II	
III			III		
II			III	II	

Jeu de mérelle

The 'jeu de mérelle' is a very old board game from the Middle Ages. Each player has 10 pieces: one has white pieces, the other has black pieces. The winner is the first one to make a line of three pieces in his own colour following the straight lines of the game board.

We are in the middle of a game between two squires, who each have a few pieces left to play. It's Eudes's turn; he's using the white pieces: where should he place his piece to be sure of winning?

Solution p. 136.

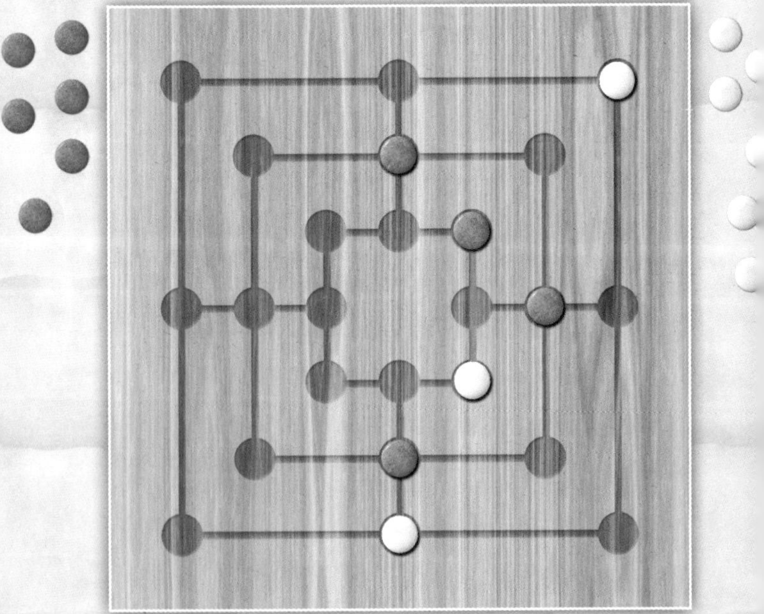

It is written

— Now here, knight, you're going to be stuck. I'm keen to give you a riddle out of Christian charity, but I'm betting you won't be able to find the solution!

Barbequiou, go get the mustard ...

> *To make its acquisition*
> *One must extract, it is said*
> *In a menacing tone*
> *From the highest place the secretion*
> *Of the sudoriparous glands.*

What on earth could it be?

Solution p. 171.

Bad at maths

Gathered around the Round Table, the knights were debating amongst themselves. Should young Perceval be knighted and welcomed among Arthur's companions?

'He's just a kid, a coarse little peasant!' grumbled Lancelot.
'A kid, but a kid who was able to vanquish the Red Knight, the same Red Knight who inflicted a shameful defeat on your seneschal, Sire!' pleaded Bors.
'A peasant's son, but one of great purity of heart added Galahad,'and I know of what I speak.'

'Very well!' said Arthur. 'Bring him in and have him pass the mad mathematics test. We will ask him how it is possible that five is half of ten, but also that seven is half of twelve and eight half of thirteen.'

'No problem,' said Perceval, 'mad mathematics is just my department — no operation has ever beaten me!'

What about you?

Solution p. 171.

Dragon steak

Barely had Tristan stepped off the boat onto Irish soil when
he found himself attacked by a formidable dragon, which he
managed to slay after an intensely fought battle, but not without
himself receiving multiple wounds. The daughter of the king of
Ireland, Iseult the Fair, comes to look after him.

'Valiant knight,' she says to him, 'to regain your strength and
recover your health, I recommend a nice dragon steak. How do
you like it? Rare, medium or well done?'
'Well done!'

However, now our fair lady finds herself in rather a fix. Because
from the outside one dragon steak looks very much like any other
dragon steak, whether it's rare, medium or well done: you can
only go on cooking time. But, and here's the ridiculous thing, she
only has two hourglasses: one that will let her cook a 'rare' dragon
steak in 13 minutes, and one for 'medium', 21 minutes. But for the
29 minutes it takes for a 'well done' steak, she has nothing.

Will Tristan have to go without his steak?

Solution p. 172.

Deluxe mustard pot

Suppose there's an empty cup.
But mind! Not just an ordinary cup, no: the cup I refer to is a metal cup, with a lid, a hanap …
And not just any size hanap: a half-pint hanap.
And not just in any metal: it's a silver-gilt hanap.
And not just any kind of silver-gilt: the silver is plated with 24-carat gold.
And the gold, it's not just any kind you know, but gold taken from the mines of Bohemia, covering silver traded in Wallachia, if you don't mind.

If there are 317 roquilles in a pint, and three drops make 1 roquille, how many drops of mead can you put in an empty hanap, the lid of which — crafty devil that you are — I just know you've lifted first?

Solution p. 172.

The solo crossing of the worm

'Cornegidouille!' Brother Gastule exclaimed. 'The little bastard! And with the price of parchment these days! The cost of what he's gobbled up is at least ... at least ...'

The little bastard was a worm which had gone in a straight line, 2 centimetres below the top margin, through a magnificent manuscript Bible in six volumes, shelved upright alongside each other, closely packed and all in order, Genesis first and the New Testament last, as can be read from the title plates on the spines.

These were six volumes that everyone to a man had thought were sufficiently protected by the wooden boards used for the covers, which were nevertheless, if you don't mind me saying, precisely 5 millimetres thick, for volumes that were 10 centimetres thick, measuring the parchment alone. A tough little bastard!

The worm started where he was born, on page 1 of the manuscript, and finished his long lunch on the last page of the New Testament.

Come now, Brother Gastule, you don't say 'he's gobbled up', but rather 'he's eaten up': and can you say what distance your bibliophile worm has covered while nourishing himself with this edifying reading?

Solution p. 172.

Puzzle

Can you reconstruct this medieval scene?

Place the pieces A, B, C, D, E and F into the squares numbered 1 to 6.

Solution p. 143.

A

B

C

D

E

F

1	2	3
4	5	6

Who does what?

On the same day there are three celebrations taking place at the castle: the knighthood of the son, Guillaume; the marriage of the daughter, Jeanne, and the return of brother Jacques. Three colours (blue, green and red) and three themes (Florence, Cyprus and Ghent) have been chosen for the celebrations organised in their honour. Which celebration does each one have, if:

- **Guillaume likes neither red nor Flanders.**
- **Jeanne shall be draped in blue.**
- **Jacques is Florentine by adoption.**

Complete the table below

Celebration for	Colour	Theme
	green	
	red	
	blue	

Solution p. 147.

Token collection

Eduald collects numbered tokens and as he has a passion for logic, he doesn't want to present his collection in any ordinary way. He has a small tray made for himself on which he can arrange his tokens in a very cunning way — in fact, without realising it, he has invented sudoku! The filling of the tray is subject to the same constraints: each number appears only once in each row, each column and in each of the 9 groups of 3x3 squares.

But Eduald has just knocked over the tray! Fortunately, to help him remember how the tokens were arranged, Eduald has marked numbers around the grid representing the sum of the numbers up to the first thicker line (towards the left, right, up or down). Can you help him put his collection back?

Solution p. 150.

68

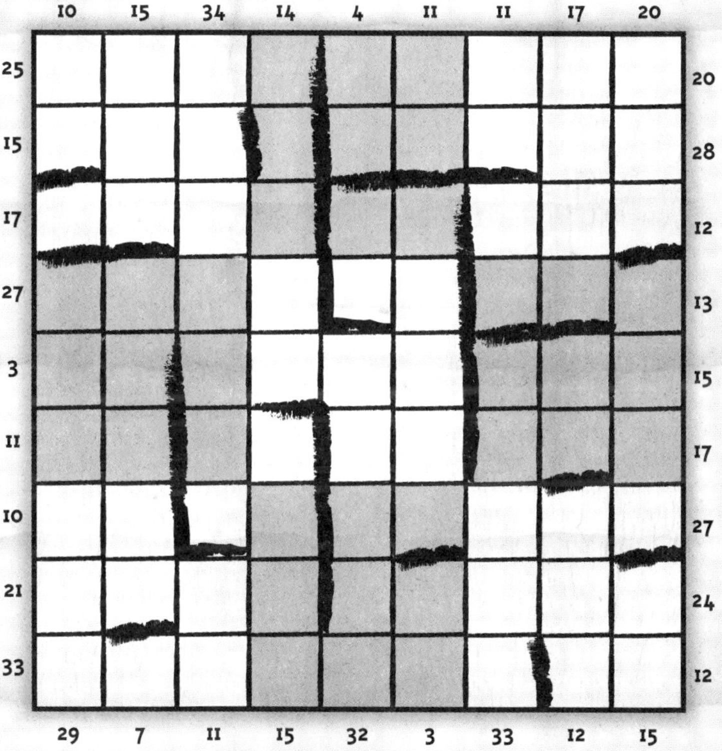

	10	15	34	14	4	11	11	17	20	
25										20
15										28
17										12
27										13
3										15
11										17
10										27
21										24
33										12
	29	7	11	15	32	3	33	12	15	

69

Name skeletons

During a memorable battle of the Hundred Years War, the soldiers lost the vowels from their first names.

Are you able to complete these name skeletons?

A warning: their name may have begun with a vowel …

Solution p. 148.

THRR

PPN

CHLDRC

SGBRT

The Fountain of the Three Maidens

The dwarf who stood before the entry to the cave didn't have the friendliest air, his speech left no avenue for appeal and the dragon lying at his feet was less than engaging.

'Noble Galahad,' he said, 'if your quest in search of marvels must pass via this cave, be aware that in order to go any further you will have to solve the mystery of the Fountain of the Three Maidens. In the middle of this cave there sits an alabaster fountain in the form of three fair young damsels. The water that spouts forth from their white bosoms bounces off their little feet with a pretty sound and then falls immediately into a bottomless pit. The mechanism that starts the fountain is activated by one of these three rings that you see here: they are all in the off position and with a half-turn to the right one of them, and only one, will get it going.'

'The test you must submit to is this: you have to work out, without going into the cave beforehand, which of these three rings activates the Fountain of the Three Maidens. The fountain is located too far inside one of the chambers of the cave for you to be able to see the least thing from here, or hear the least sound. If you give the right answer, I will disappear as if by magic. But be aware that the last knight who attempted the challenge, two years ago now, failed — my dragon made barbecue meat out of him.'

How will Galahad go about the challenge so as not to end up as a knight kebab? *Solution p. 173.*

Small potatoes

Perceval, Bors and Gawain are playing a game that's typically Welsh and totally incomprehensible. It's a game of 31 cards where you bet with diamonds. With each hand, the loser doubles the number of diamonds owned by each adversary. But if you don't have any diamonds in hand they'll take sausages. If you don't have any sausages, they'll take anything that can't be split up or divided, for example, small potatoes.

The game is so stupid and complicated that Bors and Gawain give up after five hands, and get up with the firm intention of going to bed.

'Ah, no!' exclaims Perceval. 'That was just a practice game. Everyone can go back to what they had at the beginning.'
'We don't care, it's only small potatoes.'
'Small potatoes or diamonds, it makes no difference. Lord Bors, you finished with how many small potatoes?'
'Eight.'
'And you, Sire Gawain?'
'I have nine in front of me.'
'And me, I have ten small potatoes. Therefore, at the beginning, I only had two!'

Why?

Solution p. 174.

What am I?

— You can't cross this bridge, knight, unless you answer the question asked of you. Otherwise, unless you are a very fast runner, you'll serve as a snack for my dragon. Barbequiou, be nice!

Here is my riddle:

Everyone has to have one
and I belong to one only
Taking someone else's
is punished by law.
Those who don't have one
bear the flag and the cross!
— On second thoughts, just the cross …

What on earth could it be?

Solution p. 156.

Arithmetic

Brother John is an excellent calligrapher but he's also a good mathematician. So he likes to set out mathematical operations and try to solve them. This time, he has set out the following operation, in which the different letters correspond to different values:

$$
\begin{array}{r}
\mathrm{III} \ \ \mathrm{A} \\
+ \ \ \mathrm{A} \ \ \mathrm{C} \\
\hline
\mathrm{D} \ \ \mathrm{D}
\end{array}
$$

And he wonders what the value of C must be for this operation to be correct.

Solution p. 124.

Massacres
and making love

Michaud du Potaige, responding to the call of His Holiness the Pope, leaves to go to the aid of the Eastern Christians and free the Holy Land.

He meets up with Godfrey of Bouillon in Constantinople at the end of the year 1096 and participates in the Siege of Jerusalem on 15 July 1099: the massacre of Saracens was such, they say, that one walked in blood up to the ankles.

After washing his nether-stockings and confessing his sins, the honourable Du Potaige takes his leave from Bouillon and heads back home via Venice, where he learns that during his absence his wife has died in childbirth. The child, a boy, has survived.

When he sees once again, alas, the chimney smoke of his humble village and crosses the yard of his little *château*, his jester rushes out to welcome him.

'What about my son?'
'Ah! My Lord, he is sick, in quarantine. You can't see him for three weeks.'
'Is he handsome? How old is he?'
'He is, my Lord, 32 years younger than you. And in 6 years, he will a fifth of your age.'
'No need for kid gloves,' replied the honourable du Potaige. 'I'm not the sort to bite the hand that feeds me.'

What has Godfrey of Bouillon's companion just learned?
Solution p. 175.

Money for bling

Arthur, who has a few cashflow problems, dreams that the Lady of the Lake helps him to refloat the kingdom's coffers by making him a gift of three enchanted horses, which he settles into his stables in front of a well-filled hayrack. In the morning, at matins, they are given good hay, good straw and and good grass, and the next morning, at matins once again, they get from the other end, instead of manure, solid new golden crowns.

The first horse is a bay horse, and every day he produces 250 crowns. A fifth of this is collected every morning at the feet of the second animal, a small Arab horse, who produces three times less than the third horse, called Return.

If, in his dream, Arthur has food rations for a week, how many hours and minutes will it take for him to be able to buy himself the gold hourglass he dreams of wearing as a bracelet charm to impress foreign ambassadors, and which costs a mere 270 crowns?

Solution p. 178.

Breton-style

— Who are you looking for, my lord?
— I am looking for someone whose father is the father-in-law of the father of the grandfather of my great-nephew.

Who on earth could it be?

Solution p. 178.

Forest of Figures

Lusignan Forest is a muddle of paths. To get their bearings, the woodcutters have made a map, but not so simple that any poachers who find it could easily use it.

They therefore note down on the map the number of paths that leave in different directions from particular points.

All you have to do is draw the paths that join the Roman numerals together, using this clue, in order to draw the map of this section of the forest.

Solution p. 133.

Twelve feet minus the toes

Gawain, weary and bowed down with fatigue, has had enough of wandering, Brother Gastule at his side, in search of the Green Chapel, and prays for them to be given some rest at long last. All of a sudden, at the edge of the forest, a castle set on a square lot appears as if by magic: the castle of Hautdesert. It seems to be abandoned, but should do the job for a lifesaving night of rest.

They still have to get inside, however. The castle is surrounded by a deep moat 12 feet wide that follows the edges of the square, and the knight and his sidekick, who go all the way around looking for a way to get in, don't find either a bridge or any form of boat. The water that fills the moat is packed with piranhas and stingrays — let's just say that Gawain has no desire to perform a demonstration of his butterfly stroke, and in any case he can't stand cold water.

He thus sends Brother Gastule in search of a couple of planks in order to improvise a bridge. The monk returns with two planks that are 11 feet and 12 inches long.
'Zounds, idiot! At least three toes are missing, you can see yourself that your planks are too short!'
'Nay indeed, my Lord Gawain,' says the monk, sniggering beneath his cowl, 'we'll land feet first on the other side!'

What does he have in mind?

Solution p. 176.

Knife edge

— These seven daggers, my Lord Knight, arranged on the ground in the following way, create a message that is not a message of truth.

The first two form a V, followed by two more in a vertical position, then two more in a horizontal position, one on top of the other. The seventh, finally, is in a vertical position.

Such that you can make out this preposterous equation:

VII = I

How, my Lord knight, can you make a true equation by moving just one, and only one, dagger?

Solution p. 176.

Maniac!

Here's a knight who, being punished by his lady, has been living as a hermit for 12 years right next to a chapel, nursing a very heavy heart, and his whole life is ruled by a broken clock that only chimes at 6-hour intervals. Sometimes it's 6 o'clock, sometimes it's 12. The chimes are all he hears, the chimes are all he has to look forward to; he eats his lunch timing each mouthful with the 12 strokes of midday, he can only urinate to the 6 strokes of the clock — in short — it's become an obsession not to mention very bad for the digestion.

And as he swallows things — very, very badly — the day a page sent by his lady comes to tell him that it was all a big joke, his hand grips his sword and the tension rises very quickly. Unfortunately for the emissary, midday has just begun to chime, and between the strokes of the clock, in the same way that he usually handles his fork, he sets to cutting the page up into pieces.

With the first stroke of the clock, he puts out the page's right eye, with the second stroke his left one. With the third stroke he cuts an ear off, with the fourth stroke he severs the other. Having decided to remove anything that sticks out, with the next stroke he takes to the right hand, then the left foot, the left hand, then the right foot, the left nipple, the right nipple, he cuts off the nose, and to finish off, he ...

And to finish off?

Solution p. 177.

Puzzle

Can you reconstruct this medieval scene?

Place the pieces A, B, C, D, E and F into the squares numbered 1 to 6. *Solution p. 144.*

A

B

C

D

E

F

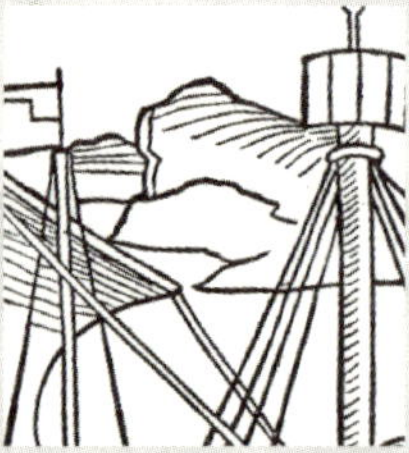

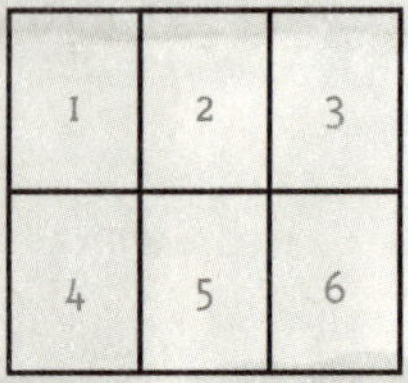

1	2	3
4	5	6

82

He who has drunk will drink again

Without wanting to be a tattletale, it's safe to say Brother Gastule is rather fond of a drink.

Opening a low sideboard, he has chanced upon a litre bottle of mead that Galahad brought back from the Castle of Maidens without partaking of any (I mean the mead), 20-years old, a pure wheat-blond wonder (I'm talking about the mead). The image of Galahad passes before Brother Gastule's rheumy eyes and draws a snigger of pity: chastity is one thing, Brother Gastule can understand that, but to spend your life sucking on spring water …

It's thus without any scruples that Brother Gastule uncorks the bottle and knocks back a large glassful, which represents one- seventh of its contents, but as he fears for his reputation, he replaces what he has drunk with spring water.

The next evening, by the most amazing chance, his path takes him in front of the same low sideboard, and he finds himself face to face with the same bottle, whose integrity he violates in the same manner: he drinks a seventh of the contents and tops it up with water so it contains a litre again.

At the end of a week of this little game, how much mead is left in the bottle?

Solution p. 178.

Token collection

Eduald collects numbered tokens and as he has a passion for logic, he doesn't want to present his collection in any ordinary way. He has a small tray made for himself on which he can arrange his tokens in a very cunning way — in fact, without realising it, he has invented sudoku! The filling of the tray is subject to the same constraints: each number appears only once in each row, each column and in each of the 9 groups of 3x3 squares.

But Eduald has just knocked over the tray! Fortunately, to help him remember how the tokens were arranged, Eduald has marked numbers around the grid representing the sum of the numbers up to the first thicker line (towards the left, right, up or down). Can you help him put his collection back?

Solution p. 151.

	16	15	29	15	6	8	17	17	14	
18										27
18										21
18										11
21										15
15										13
8										17
9										25
22										23
35										10
	25	3	16	18	31	5	18	11	17	

Chivalry
and handicaps

These five propostions are true:

1. No wandering knight on foot collects mushrooms.
2. No wandering knight without armour goes backwards.
3. Wandering knights carring a sword always collect mushrooms.
4. No wandering knight on horseback stutters.
5. All wandering knights wearing armour carry a sword.

Do wandering knights who stutter go backwards?

Solution p. 177.

Fiddling the figures

Let's remind ourselves of the Roman numerals:

I	5	10	50	100	500	1000
I	V	X	L	C	D	M

If you write the number 5500 in Roman numerals, and then take just one of each Roman numeral used, what new number do you get?

Solution p. 154.

At the Castle of Pesme-Aventure

After defeating Harpin of the Mountain, an evil giant dressed in bear skins, Ywain, the Knight of the Lion, still had to face the malevolent sorcery of the Castle of Pesme-Aventure. 'You won't be able to leave,' its owners had told him, 'unless you fight and win against the demonic creatures that haunt our dwelling!'

After killing two monstrous sergeants, Lord Ywain was, as if by magic, surrounded by a horde of 63 hideous green goblins armed with axes and daggers. He unsheathed his sword, struck to his right, sliced to his left, and by wildly waving his arms around quickly managed to cut down those who came within reach: in short, he exterminated all of the goblins, with the exception of two he had only wounded and who his faithful lion finished off at his own pace, two cripples who slipped away via a secret staircase that led to the kitchens, while the ground was strewn with slices of goblin marinating in pools of blood as green as mint leaves.

How many goblins are left?

Solution p. 178.

Abacus

This is an abacus reset to zero. To represent a number, you move the beads towards the centre beam. Only the beads next to the centre beam are counted.

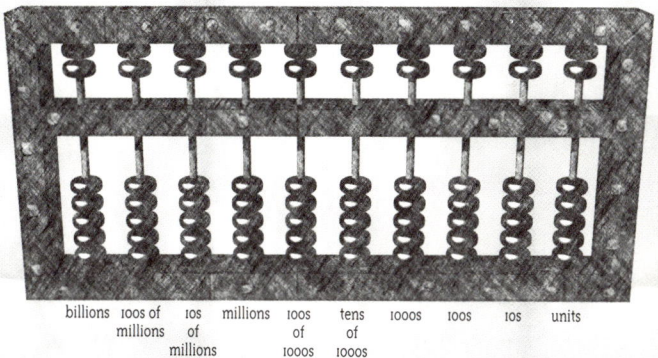

| billions | 100s of millions | 10s of millions | millions | 100s of 1000s | tens of 1000s | 1000s | 100s | 10s | units |

⊘ = 5

⊘ = 1

If I add 147 210 652 to this abacus, what is the new abacus arrangement that results?

Solution p. 127.

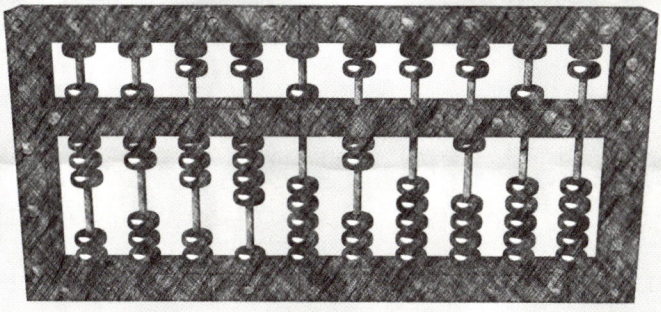

The value of things

A family sells sheep's milk cheeses. At midday the father has sold 40 cheeses while the mother has sold 22. The son and daughter have sold some as well. In the afternoon, each member of the family has sold 14 cheeses. At the end of the day the father has sold double the number of the son; the mother and daughter have sold 100.

How many cheeses did the children sell in the morning?

Solution p. 137.

The drakkars

You have to work out the position of the Norman drakkars using the coordinate grid on the opposite page. The figures indicate the number of squares in the row or column occupied by a ship. Watch out! Each boat is surrounded by water (two boats can't touch each other). To help you, we have identified a few empty squares. The reefs prevent anyone from navigating through there.

You have to find:

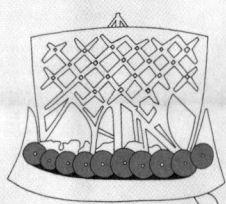

◻◻◻◻ 3 large drakkars
◻◻◻ 5 skeiðs
◻◻ 4 snekkjas
◻ 2 longboats

Solution p. 140.

	4	3	2	6	3	1	4	3	3	5	3	
												4
												1
												6
												2
												4
												3
												1
												4
												0
												4
												4
												3
												1

Graeco-Latin square

Remember that a magic square is an ancestor of sudoku: there are 4 numbers in a 4 × 4 grid, but each occurs only once in each row, each column and each diagonal.

This Graeco-Latin square is made up of two magic squares combined together and 'superimposed' on each other. You have to separate them to work out the two original grids.

Solution p. 131.

CCI	MML	CXX	XII
XXX	CII	CCL	MMI
LII	XXI	MMX	CCC
MMC	CCX	III	LXX

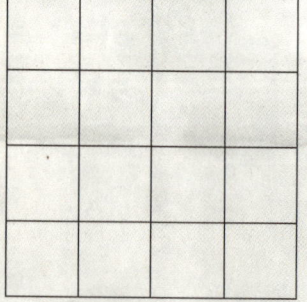

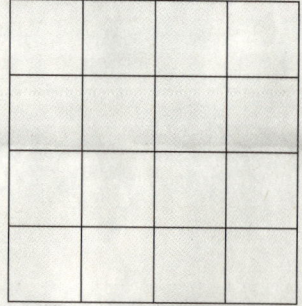

Puzzle

Can you reconstruct this medieval scene?

Place the pieces A, B, C, D, E and F into the squares numbered 1 to 6.

Solution p. 145.

A

B

C

D

E

F

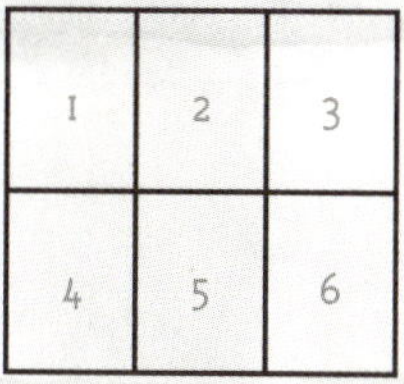

1	2	3
4	5	6

Name skeletons

During a memorable battle of the Hundred Years War, the soldiers lost the vowels from their first names.

Are you able to complete these name skeletons?

A warning: their name may have begun with a vowel ...

Solution p. 148.

FLVN

DS

GTN

GSPRD

Tormented souls

Brother Gastule takes himself to an empty chapel close to the Fountain of the Green Lady, a place of pilgrimage especially popular with young women who have made bad marriages. Our good friend the monk, as you may imagine, has other fish to fry, but he's not above mixing with the good citizenry.

Regarding which, along the way he crosses the paths of five litters carried by four valets. Each of the litters carries a damsel of gentle birth, accompanied by two jesters or minstrels to distract her from her melancholy during the trip. The two jesters in the third litter are in fact Siamese twins of the dicephalic type, which is to say that two heads share the same body.

How many people will thus end up at the disused chapel?

Solution p. 179.

Token collection

Eduald collects numbered tokens and as he has a passion for logic, he doesn't want to present his collection in any ordinary way. He has a small tray made for himself on which he can arrange his tokens in a very cunning way — in fact, without realising it, he has invented sudoku! The filling of the tray is subject to the same constraints: each number appears only once in each row, each column and in each of the 9 groups of 3x3 squares.

But Eduald has just knocked over the tray! Fortunately, to help him remember how the tokens were arranged, Eduald has marked numbers around the grid representing the sum of the numbers up to the first thicker line (towards the left, right, up or down). Can you help him put his collection back?

Solution p. 152.

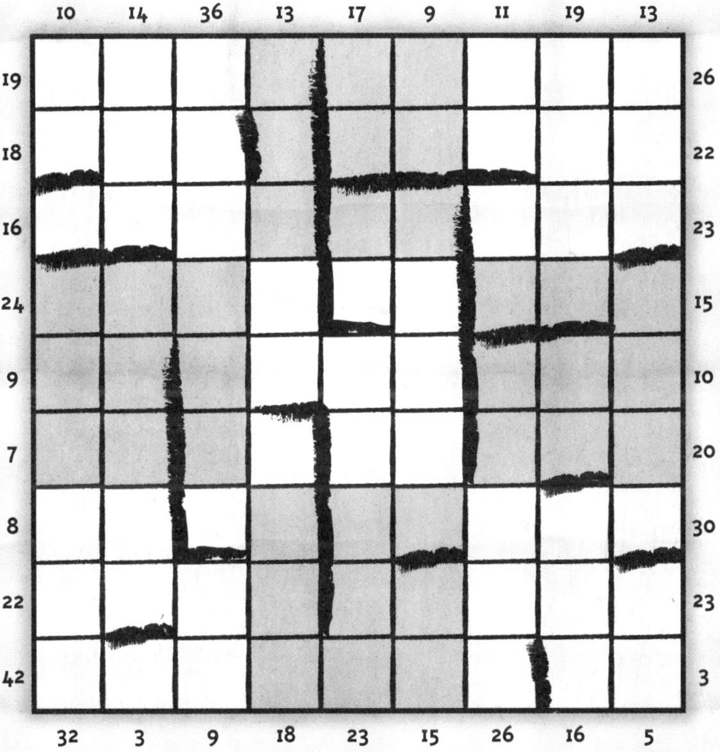

	10	14	36	13	17	9	11	19	13	
19										26
18										22
16										23
24										15
9										10
7										20
8										30
22										23
42										3
	32	3	9	18	23	15	26	16	5	

Wool over their eyes

The room was square, one of those vast castle rooms, icy as you like. Sitting in each corner was a monk dressed in a habit, looking only half awake, his cowl down over his eyes — in other words, with the wool pulled down over his eyes.

And sitting in front of each of these monks were four other monks, the wool pulled down over their eyes.

Unless you're also feeling a bit woolly-headed, you'll already have counted the number of monks in this square room with the wool pulled down over their eyes.

Solution p. 179.

Fiddling the figures

Let's remind ourselves of the Roman numerals:

I	**5**	**10**	**50**	**100**	**500**	**1000**
I	**V**	**X**	**L**	**C**	**D**	**M**

The number 44 is a palindrome in Arabic numerals — it reads the same way from left to right and from right to left. If you write it in Roman numerals, and then take just one of each Roman numeral used, what new palindrome in Arabic numerals can you make?

Solution p. 154.

Aucassin and Nicole

Aucassin and Nicole are very much in love and are therefore inseparable. Wherever Aucassin is, Nicole is by his side. Each Aucassin ✖ thus has beside him a Nicole ▼.

The rules:

The figures above the columns and in front of the rows indicate the number of times Nicole ▼ appears there. Find the 18 Nicoles hidden in the grid, if:

• There are as many Aucassins ✖ as Nicoles ▼.
• Each square containing a ▼ must be paired, on one of its sides, by a square containing a ✖.
• Two squares containing a ▼ can't touch each other either by the sides or the corners.   *Solution p. 126.*

	3	2	2	2	3	2	2	2
3	✖					✖		
0	✖				✖			✖
4			✖				✖	
0	✖							
3				✖				
0			✖			✖		
4	✖						✖	
0				✖				
0	✖							
4		✖		✖		✖		

Graeco-Latin square

Remember that a magic square is an ancestor of sudoku: there are 4 numbers in a 4 × 4 grid, but each occurs only once in each row, each column and each diagonal.

This Graeco-Latin square is made up of two magic squares combined together and 'superimposed' on each other. You have to separate them to work out the two original grids.

Clue: the Cs stay together.

Solution p. 131.

XCV	CXIV	MCCVII	XVI
XVII	MCCVI	CXV	XCIV
CXVI	XCVII	XIV	MCCV
MCCIV	XV	XCVII	CXVII

The value of things

If I tell you that three bags of acorns is worth two bags of flour plus one bag of acorns ...

Can you tell me how many bags of acorns I need for a bag of flour?

Solution p. 138.

The drakkars

You have to work out the position of the Norman drakkars using the coordinate grid on the opposite page. The figures indicate the number of squares in the row or column occupied by a ship. Watch out! Each boat is surrounded by water (2 boats can't touch each other). To help you, we have identified a few empty squares. The reefs prevent anyone from navigating through there.

You have to find:

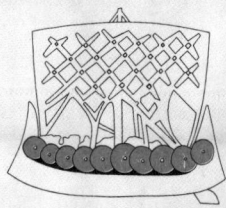

▢▢▢▢   4 large drakkars
▢▢▢   4 skeiðs
▢▢   4 snekkjas
▢   4 longboats

Solution p. 140.

	3	5	2	6	2	4	6	2	4	2	4	
												2
												6
												2
												3
												2
												6
												1
												5
												1
												4
												1
												3
												4

Not the hair

— I won't let you pass, knight, unless you are able to answer the question I give you. Otherwise, I'll hand you over to my dragon. Barbequiou, heel!

Here is my riddle:

You hold me without touching me
If you lose me you can't ask for me back

What on earth could it be?

Solution p. 179.

A race against the grain

'I want to offer a reward to your friends, who have come to my aid even though they have nothing in common with our line. It is a great reward, but it cannot be divided. See this cauldron: it is magic. It's a cauldron that bestows life.'

The scene is taking place at Corbenic Castle, where the Fisher King has just been cured of a paralysing injury by his nephew Perceval, accompanied by the knights Bors and Galahad.

'Now, then!' continues the king. 'You're going to compete in a race ... but a race worthy of a wounded king, an impotent king: rather than the first, it will be the last one whose horse reaches the Dolmen of the Wasteland who will be the winner!'

Barely has he finished speaking than Bors has already disappeared at a great gallop in a cloud of dust, with Galahad hot on his heels, digging in the spurs.

'Idiots!' curses the Fisher King. 'They've completely missed the point!'
'No, they haven't, My Lord, they haven't! They've understood perfectly!' protests Perceval.

How can Perceval be right?

Solution p. 180.

Bag of tricks

In the pursuit of the murderer of his cousin's friend, Perceval meets a damsel in ragged clothing riding a scrawny and snotty-nosed horse. Perceval, who is not the kind to ask questions, would have happily continued on his way, but the maiden corners him and tells him her story.

She has been punished, she tells him, by her jealous husband, the Orgueilleux de la Lande, because he caught her giving a kiss to a Welsh manservant. It's a miracle, moreover, that she's still alive!

'Imagine, sire, we were alone that evening, warming ourselves in front of the hearth. My husband suddenly takes out his sword and presents me with two scraps of paper, completely identical. He tells me he has written on one of them "I die", and on the other "I live", then he rolls up each of the parchments, ties them up and puts them both in a leather bag, which he hands to me. Depending on which one I pull out, he will be using his sword or not ...'

'You were lucky, then!' Perceval exclaims.
'Lucky? Nay indeed! Because I clearly saw, when he wrote the message on the parchment, that the traitor wrote on both of them "I die" ...'

How is it, then, that the damsel is still of this world?

Solution p. 180.

She'll be apples

Lancelot is spending his fifteenth year tooling around on the Isle of Avalon, not even a suburb of Camelot, and totally bored. It's a time when there's no motor scooters and no games consoles, no bus shelters to break or cars to burn. The adolescent, bored as a dead cormorant and finding himself in some typical Briton mizzle on the Isle of Avalon with only the cromlech on the Tor for amusement, is a hair's breadth from depression and that's very bad for his growth.

Our future precocious depressive has found nothing better to do than kick an apple tree to make apples fall, and when he has finished taking out his boredom on the tree, he counts the apples. He counts 397 of them.

Just then the priestesses of Ceridwen, goddess of fertility, pass by, and they leap on the green fruits like a band of Venuses or Eves. Those who get in first take 5 each, and there's one-sixth of the group left who can only take away one each, with the exception of three lucky ones who are able to gather up 3 each.

'That's a whole lot of priestesses!' Lancelot says to himself, spitting out the pips of the one apple he managed to salvage from the raid. How many priestesses, in fact?

Solution p. 181.

Token collection

Eduald collects numbered tokens and as he has a passion for logic, he doesn't want to present his collection in any ordinary way. He has a small tray made for himself on which he can arrange his tokens in a very cunning way — in fact, without realising it, he has invented sudoku! The filling of the tray is subject to the same constraints: each number appears only once in each row, each column and in each of the 9 groups of 3x3 squares.

But Eduald has just knocked over the tray! Fortunately, to help him remember how the tokens were arranged, Eduald has marked numbers around the grid representing the sum of the numbers up to the first thicker line (towards the left, right, up or down). Can you help him put his collection back?

Solution p. 153.

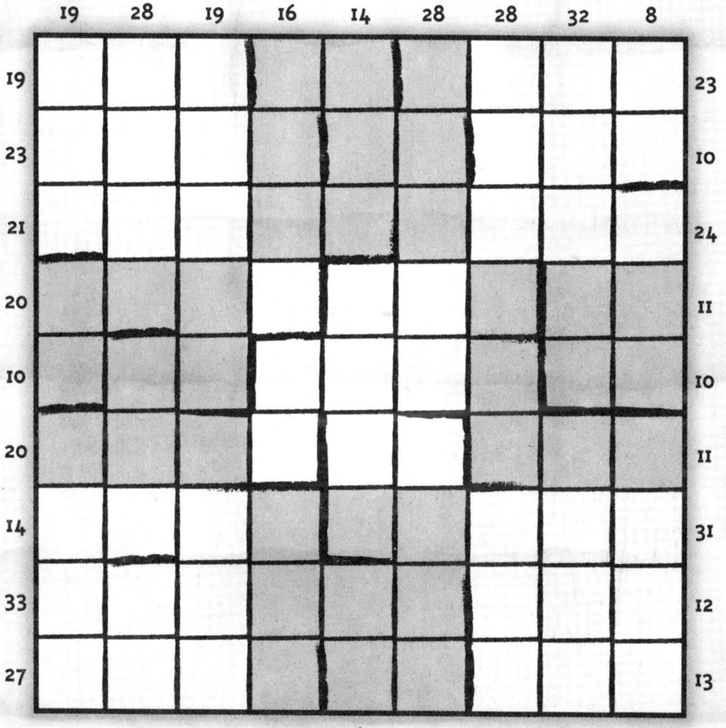

	19	28	19	16	14	28	28	32	8	
19										23
23										10
21										24
20										11
10										10
20										11
14										31
33										12
27										13
	21	9	22	22	6	17	10	13	30	

Name skeletons

During a memorable battle of the Hundred Years War, the soldiers lost the vowels from their first names.

Are you able to complete these name skeletons?

A warning: their name may have begun with a vowel ...

Solution p. 148.

RL

THBLD

PRRCK

BDN

The star

— About-turn, knight, unless you agree to take up the challenge I shall set you, in the form of a riddle. If you solve it, I will let you cross my lands. If you fail, I will set my dragon on your heels.

Here is my riddle:

Five hundred on the left and five hundred on the right
As many as the chariots captured from the army at Zobah
And five in the middle like the points of a star
Or like the five letters that spell my name

What on earth could it be?

Solution p. 182.

One-upmanship

'I saw the cocodrile and his dreadful jaws all studded with sharp teeth like a portcullis.'

'I saw the catoblepas, and his hideous, heavy face, so heavy, sires, that it drags along the ground as he plods along step by step.'

'I saw the basilisk, whose fetid breath is enough to knock whoever encounters it out cold.'

'I saw, with my own eyes, the terrible Gorgon with hair of serpents. And her gaze, sires, turns you into a statue.'

'Me, I saw the Simurgh, with rainbow feathers, and I saw the phoenix who sets itself on fire then is reborn from its ashes.'

'And I,' says Perceval, 'I saw those who were born on the same day of the same month of the same year, and to the same mother!'

'Twins then?'

'No, not twins!'

'Merciful God, Lord Perceval, what terrible monster is this, sign of great misfortune and malediction?'

Just as Perceval was about to reply — you won't believe the bad luck — he was struck by laryngitis as suddenly as a sea hawk swoops on a scorpionfish, and now he's unable to speak.

In other words, the Knights of the Round Table are counting on your insight.

Solution p. 182.

Abacus

This is an abacus reset to zero. To represent a number, you move the beads towards the centre beam. Only the beads next to the centre beam are counted.

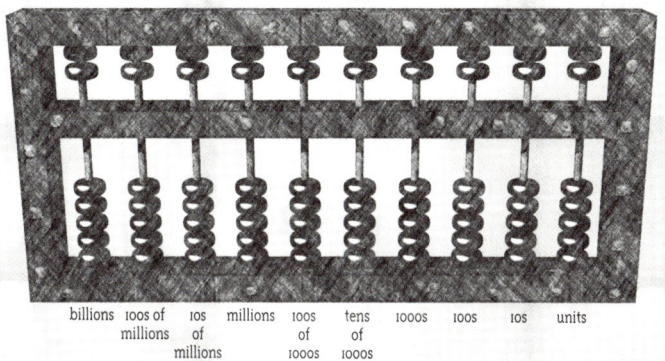

| billions | 100s of millions | 10s of millions | millions | 100s of 1000s | tens of 1000s | 1000s | 100s | 10s | units |

If I add 147 210 652 to this abacus, what is the new abacus arrangement that results?

Solution p. 128.

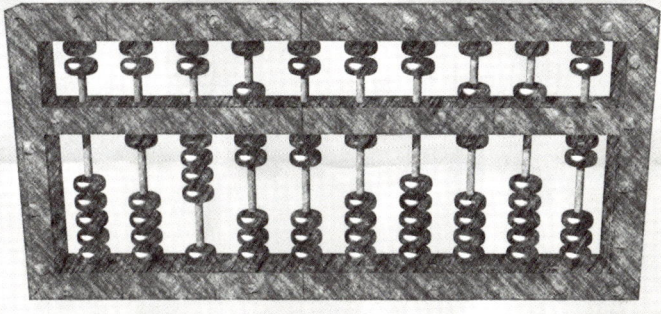

113

Friendship
and sausages

Lancelot, Bors, Galahad and Perceval find themselves in a tavern in the Rupelloux region and have decided to try the local specialties.

The staff suggest oysters. Lancelot orders five dozen oysters to be opened for him; Bors wants six dozen; Galahad, who would eat a horse, demands nine dozen; and Perceval, who's not in a very oyster mood, orders ten sausages. They get stuck into a pitcher of terrible pale barley ale, a local brew, pay in advance and wait for their order to arrive.

The innkeeper brings a platter with everything put on it together, saying they can work it out for themselves and not to be sniffy — in these parts we eat oysters with sausage. Galahad's, Bors' and Lancelot's tastebuds quiver as they inhale the aroma of the sausages while Perceval, finally seduced by the lure of the exotic, casts longing looks towards the oysters. To make it simple, his three friends decide to split the oysters into four equal portions, and Perceval, misty-eyed with gratitude and not really wanting to mix his foods, gives them all of his sausages, each receiving an amount proportionate to the sacrifice they have made.

Everyone looks happy, except for Lancelot, who starts to make a face as long as a wet weekend.
A bad oyster, perhaps?

Solution p. 182.

Restrictions

— Come down off your horse, knight, and listen carefully to my question. Who, between me and my dragon, is going to eat you alive?

No, just kidding. Here's my riddle:

> *Nuns don't use one in principle*
> *The Pope doesn't either, though he has one*
> *But your father's is used by your mother*

What on earth could it be?

Solution p. 180.

The drakkars

You have to work out the position of the Norman drakkars using the coordinate grid on the opposite page. The figures indicate the number of squares in the row or column occupied by a ship. Watch out! Each boat is surrounded by water (two boats can't touch each other). To help you, we have identified a few empty squares. The reefs prevent anyone from navigating through there.

You have to find:

❑❑❑❑ 4 large drakkars
❑❑❑ 4 skeiðs
❑❑ 6 snekkjas
❑ 5 longboats

Solution p. 140.

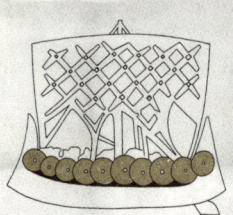

7   I   5   4   3   4   5   3   4   4   5

6

0

8

I

4

2

2

7

3

3

I

7

I

Marketing

The giant Myndyorownbyznesse has decided to breed dragons, a promising small business which should allow all the Perilous Deserts and other Desolate Forests to properly kit themselves out, a matter of spicing up the lives of the wandering knights in search of feats and giving them tales to tell to Father Blaise when they get back to Camelot.

Our giant has put together a small stock of 12 breeding dragons in perfect working order, which eat 36 wandering knights every 18 days. Among these 12 dragons, the 9 females lay on average 12 eggs every 8 days.

How many wandering knights does the giant Myndyorownbyznesse need to bump off just for his female dragons in order to produce the 150 dragon eggs he has down on order to date?

Solution p. 183.

Name skeletons

During a memorable battle of the Hundred Years War, the soldiers lost the vowels from their first names.

Are you able to complete these name skeletons?

A warning: their name may have begun with a vowel ...

Solution p. 148.

RBN

BRNGR

CLMT

TNCRD

Question for a champion

The most deserving knight — was it Perceval? was it Galahad? — the purest of the pure, the champion of champions, had almost reached the end of the supreme quest. He already had the Spear of Longinus and he came to a halt before a table on which, as if on an altar, a venerable hand had placed four recipients, four cups, all very different from each other. One of them, so the Fisher King had foretold him, was the Grail, the holy chalice with which Christ celebrated the Last Supper and in which his blood had been collected after his sacrifice!

The Holy Grail ... But which of the four cups was it?

Then a lugubrious voice boomed out, uttering these words: 'Come closer, knight, and read. Each of these cups bears an inscription. Understand that one, and only one, of these inscriptions is true. Read, and make your choice. If you correctly identify the Grail, you will have eternal life. If you are mistaken, tough luck.'

On the first cup, which was made of copper, was written: 'This is not the Grail.'
On the second cup, made of silver, was written: 'This is the Grail.'
On the third, made of iron, was written: 'The silver cup is not the Grail.'
On the fourth, made of gold, was written: 'The iron cup is the Grail.'
Which cup will the knight choose?

Solution p. 162.

Variation on a theme

— I won't give you the keys to the cell, knight, unless you solve the riddle. Otherwise, I'll bring in my dragon.
Barbequiou, stay outside, sit!

After killing his father, marrying his mother and putting out his own eyes, Œdipus runs into his old mate the Sphinx. Instead of killing herself, as the story almost always goes, the Sphinx of Thebes had actually gone off quietly to talk in riddles somewhere else and then turned up again incognito in Boeotia. Œdipus finds her at apéritif hour and, sucking on a few olives, asks her, cool as you like:

What has four legs in the morning, two at midday and three in the evening?

What on earth could it be?

Solution p. 183.

Solutions

Arithmetic

PAGE 10

Solution

It doesn't much matter, it's arm length that will be the deciding factor!

PAGE 52

Solution

A = 9

C = 8 and B = 2

29 + 82 + 888 = 999

Explanation

A + B + C = A means that B + C = 10 and that 1 is carried over to the previous column.

B + C + 8 + 1 (carried over) = A and 1 carried over once again. But if B + C = 10, therefore A=9 and there is 1 carried over to the previous column.

C + 1 (carried over) = A = 9 means C = 8 and we can therefore deduce that B = 2.

PAGE 74

Solution

What is most certain is that C is equal to 3 and that there's no carry-over when you add up A + C = D, and it must also be the case then that A is less than 7.

Aucassin and Nicole

	2	2	3	1	3	2	3	2
3		✖	▼		▼		▼	✖
1	▼	✖			✖	✖		✖
3		✖	▼			▼		▼
0								
3	✖	▼			✖	▼	✖	▼
0								
3	✖	▼	✖	▼	✖	▼		
1								▼
1	▼	✖	✖		✖			✖
3			▼		▼	✖	▼	

Method

Cancel out the 2 rows where there is no Nicole and complete the fifth row, then the first three ... When you feel blocked completing a row, look at the clues for the columns (and vice versa).

	3	2	2	2	3	2	2	2
3	✖	▼			▼	✖	▼	
0	✖				✖			✖
4	▼		✖	▼		▼	✖	▼
0	✖							
3	▼		▼	✖	▼			
0			✖			✖		
4	✖	▼		▼		▼	✖	▼
0				✖				
0	✖							
4	▼	✖	▼	✖	▼	✖	▼	

Method

Cancel out the 5 rows where there is no Nicole and complete the third row, then the last and the first column … When you feel blocked completing the rows, look at the clues for the columns (and vice versa).

Abacus

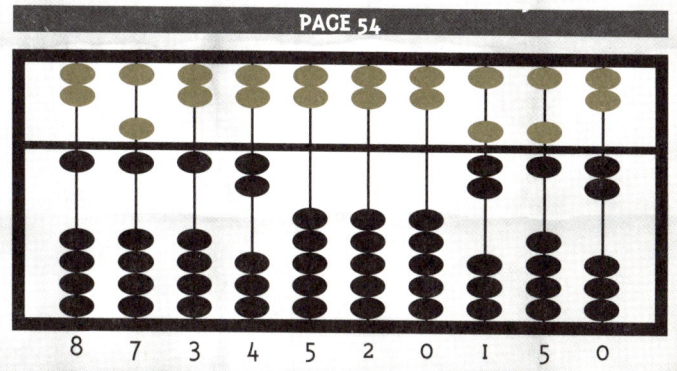

8 7 3 4 5 2 0 1 5 0

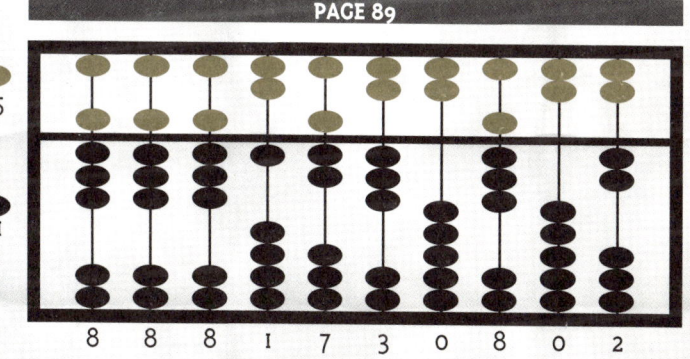

8 8 8 1 7 3 0 8 0 2

127

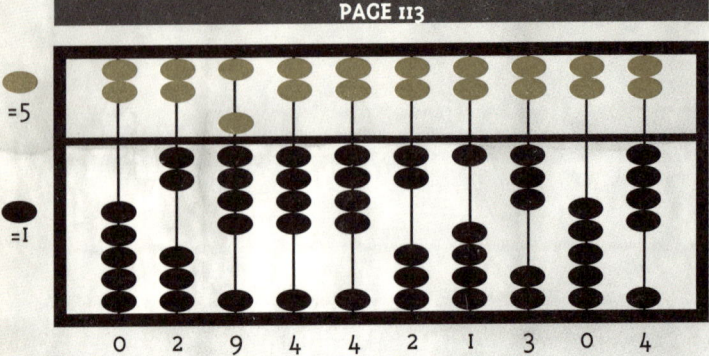

=5

=1

0 2 9 4 4 2 1 3 0 4

Pigments

Naples Yellow
Rouen Green
German Black
Brazilian Red
Egyptian Blue
Saint John's White

Forest of figures

You have to start with the IV cards: this means that this point is an intersection of 4 paths.

Graeco-Latin square

I	V	II	III
III	II	V	I
V	I	III	II
II	III	I	V

C	X	XX	L
XX	L	C	X
L	XX	X	C
X	C	L	XX

L	X	I	C
C	I	X	L
X	L	C	I
I	C	L	X

CC	II	XX	MM
XX	MM	CC	II
MM	XX	II	CC
II	CC	MM	XX

PAGE 92

I	L	C	X
X	C	L	I
L	I	X	C
C	X	I	L

CC	MM	XX	II
XX	II	CC	MM
II	XX	MM	CC
MM	CC	II	XX

PAGE 101

XC	CX	MCC	X
X	MCC	CX	XC
CX	XC	X	MCC
MCC	X	XC	CX

V	IV	VII	VI
VII	VI	V	IV
VI	VII	IV	V
IV	V	VII	VII

Carousel

Solution

The Knight on square A1 goes to B3. The one on square C1 goes to A2. The one on square C3 goes to B1. The Knight on square A3 goes to C2. And they keep going around. From A2 to C3, from B1 to A3, from B3 to C1 and from C2 to A1.

Forest of Figures

When III and II meet up there may be a dead-end…

Watch out for the double path...

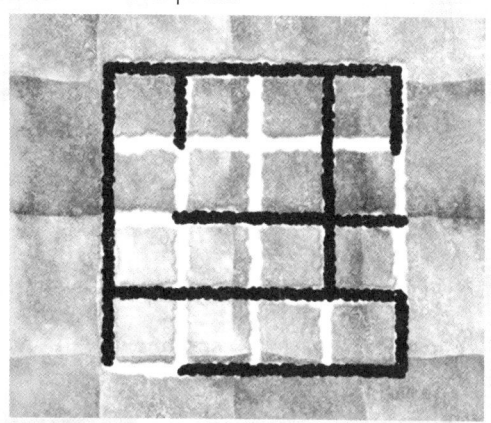

There are lots of clearings....

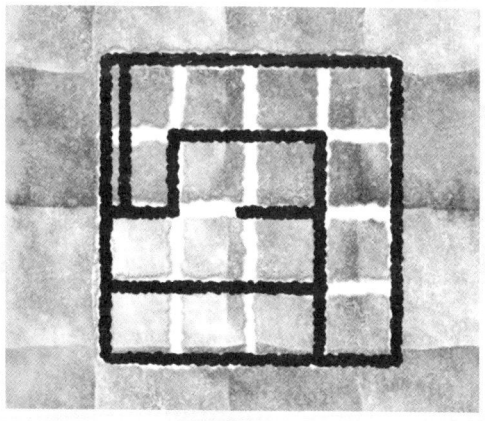

133

Jeu de mérelle

PAGE 19

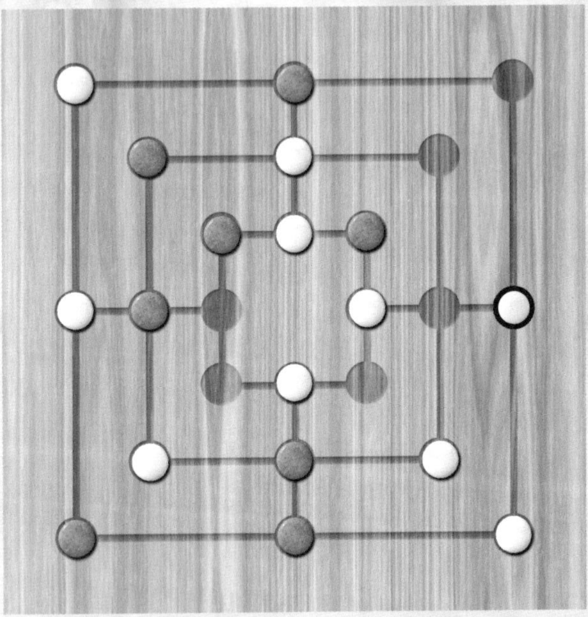

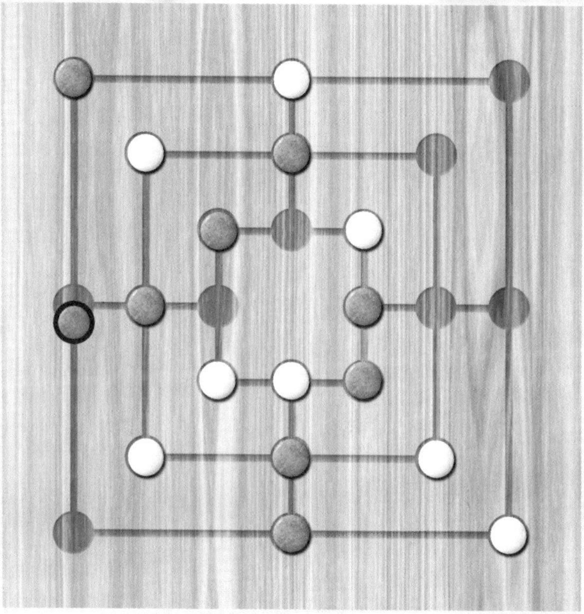

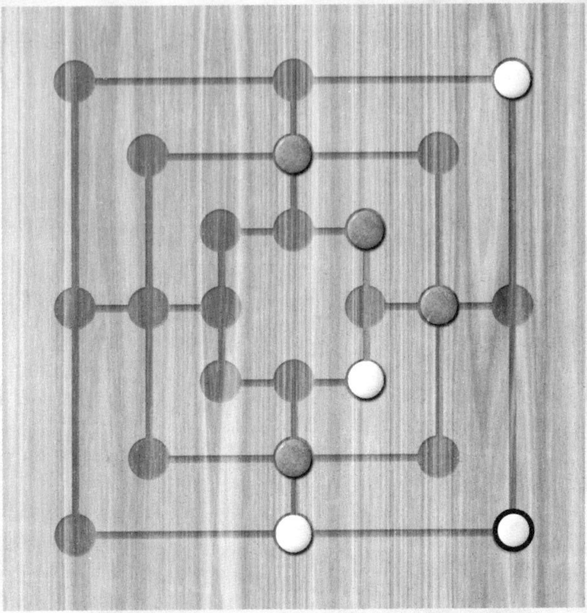

The value of things

Solution
12 days

Explanation
If d is the number of required days

30 + j = 2 (9+j) therefore j = 30 – 18 = 12

Solution
63: the son sold 13 and the daughter 50.

Explanation
At the end of the day, the total amount sold by the father is double that of the son, with 14 extra cheeses sold:
40 + 14 = 54
thus the son has sold 27 in the day.

At midday the son had thus sold:
27 – 14 = 13.

The amount sold by the mother at the end of the day is:
22 + 14 = 36
and so that of the daughter:
100 – 36 = 64.

At midday, the daughter had thus sold 50 cheeses.

Solution

One bag of acorns (A)= one bag of flour (F)

(F + F) + A = A + A + A

You just need to remove one bag of acorns from each side of the equation.

The minstrel

Solution:

The town is Aachen, otherwise known as Aix-La-Chapelle.

A. Victory in Aquitaine 770

A. Charlemagne reigns alone over the kingdom of Franks 771

C. Submission of the Lombards 774

H. Charlemagne is crowned Holy Emperor 800

E. Submission of the Saxons 804

N. Canonisation 1165

The drakkars

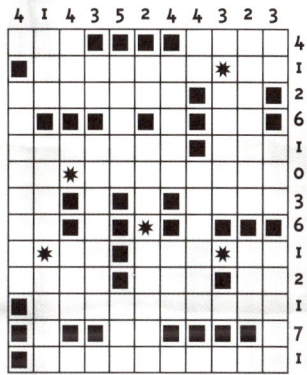

PAGE 90

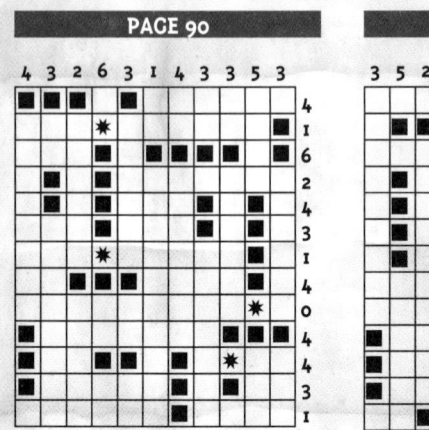

PAGE 102

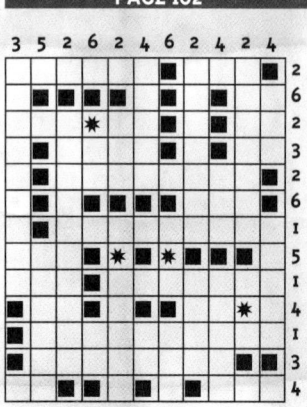

PAGE 116

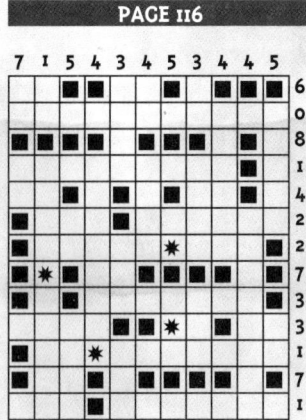

Puzzle

F

A

D

B

C

E

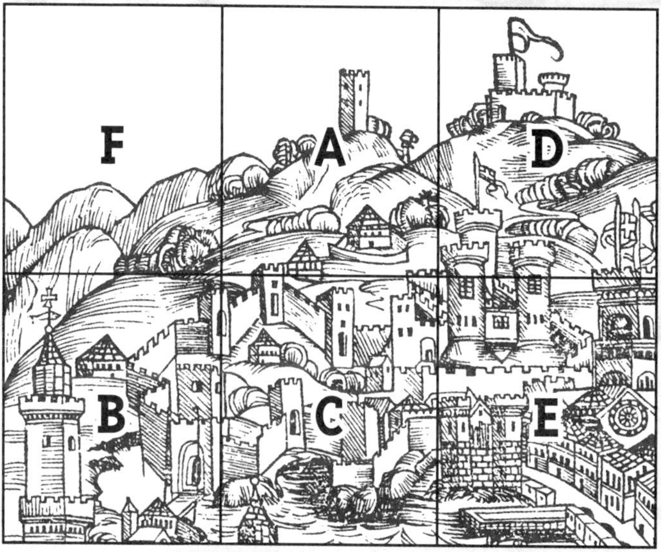

1 = F
2 = A
3 = D
4 = B
5 = C
6 = E

F C B

A D E

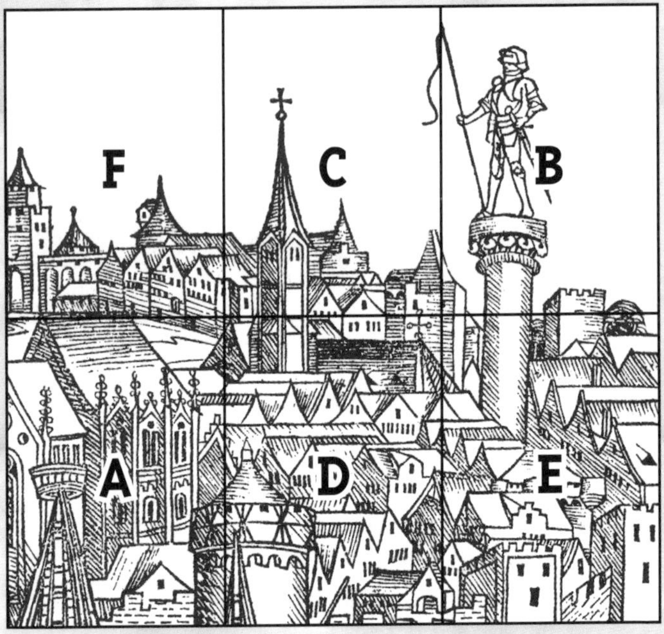

1 = F
2 = C
3 = B
4 = A
5 = D
6 = E

1 = C
2 = A
3 = E
4 = F
5 = B
6 = D

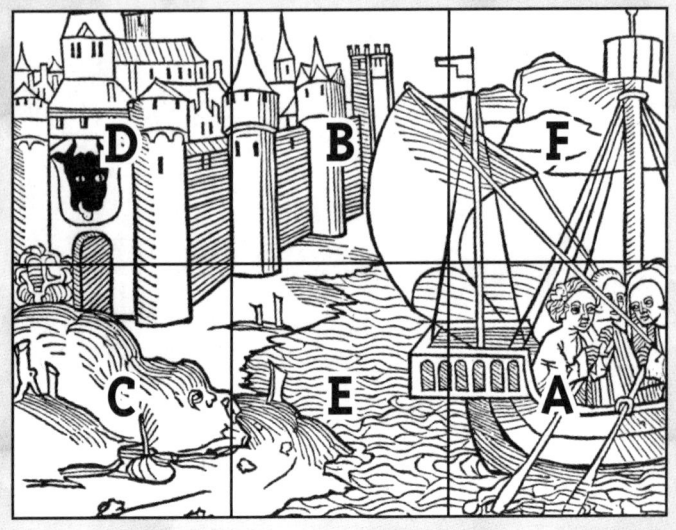

1 = D
2 = B
3 = F
4 = C
5 = E
6 = A

1 = B
2 = C
3 = D
4 = F
5 = A
6 = E

Who does what?

Name	Instrument	Result
Brother John	rock	crushed thumb
Brother William	teeth	broken tooth
Brother François	knife	cut forefinger

Explanation

'Brother John has no knife': he therefore uses his teeth or a rock. 'Brother William doesn't injure his fingers': he therefore uses his teeth and consequently Brother John uses the rock, with which he crushes his thumb, and Brother François the knife, with which he cuts his forefinger. We can deduce that Brother William breaks his tooth.

Name	Trade	Lieu
Angelin	dairyman	Saint-Barnabé market
Berenger	furrier	Lombardy market
Clodomir	draper	Saint Omer market

Explanation

Angelin sells milk so he is the dairyman. Clodomir is not a furrier, so he is the draper and goes neither to Saint-Barnabé nor to Lombardy.

Celebration for	Colour	Theme
Guillaume	green	Cyprus
Jacques	red	Florence
Jeanne	blue	Ghent

Name skeletons

Token collections

	4	15	41	10	11	10	10	19	14	
20	3	4	8	5	9	7	1	6	2	25
14	1	6	7	4	2	3	9	8	5	27
17	9	5	2	1	6	8	4	3	7	14
23	5	1	9	8	7	4	6	2	3	11
9	7	2	6	9	3	5	8	4	1	13
11	8	3	4	6	1	2	7	5	9	21
11	4	7	5	2	8	9	3	1	6	27
24	6	8	3	7	5	1	2	9	4	21
30	2	9	1	3	4	6	5	7	8	15
	32	9	4	18	21	7	25	17	12	

149

	10	15	34	14	4	11	11	17	20	
25	7	9	5	4	3	6	2	1	8	20
15	3	4	8	2	1	5	9	6	7	28
17	6	2	1	8	7	9	3	4	5	12
27	9	5	6	7	2	3	1	8	4	13
3	2	1	4	9	6	8	7	5	3	15
11	8	3	7	1	5	4	9	6	2	17
10	4	6	3	5	9	7	8	2	1	27
21	1	8	9	3	4	2	5	7	6	24
33	5	7	2	6	8	1	4	3	9	12
	29	7	11	15	32	3	33	12	15	

	16	15	29	15	6	8	17	17	14	
18	9	2	6	1	4	3	8	5	7	27
18	7	8	3	6	2	5	9	4	1	21
18	4	5	1	8	7	9	3	2	6	11
21	3	4	5	9	1	8	7	6	2	15
15	6	9	2	3	5	7	1	8	4	13
8	1	7	8	4	6	2	5	9	3	17
9	8	1	4	7	9	6	2	3	5	25
22	5	6	9	2	3	1	4	7	8	23
35	2	3	7	5	8	4	6	1	9	10
	25	3	16	18	31	5	18	11	17	

151

	10	14	36	13	17	9	11	19	13	
19	2	9	7	1	8	6	4	5	3	26
18	8	4	6	5	9	3	7	1	2	22
16	3	1	5	7	4	2	6	9	8	23
24	7	8	3	6	1	5	2	4	9	15
9	4	5	2	8	7	9	1	3	6	10
7	1	6	9	2	3	4	8	7	5	20
8	6	2	4	3	5	1	9	8	7	30
22	5	7	1	9	2	8	3	6	4	23
42	9	3	8	4	6	7	5	2	1	3
	32	3	9	18	23	15	26	16	5	

	19	28	19	16	14	28	28	32	8	
19	8	9	2	1	3	5	6	7	4	23
23	6	4	1	8	9	7	5	2	3	10
21	5	7	3	4	2	6	8	9	1	24
20	2	8	7	3	4	1	9	6	5	11
10	3	1	6	5	7	9	4	8	2	10
20	9	5	4	2	6	8	3	1	7	11
14	1	2	5	6	8	3	7	4	9	31
33	4	6	9	7	5	2	1	3	8	12
27	7	3	8	9	1	4	2	5	6	13
	21	9	22	22	6	17	10	13	30	

153

Fiddling the figures

Solution
1166

Explanation
1968 = MCMLXVIII
So the Roman numerals that make it up are
M, C, L, X, V, I
which makes MCLXVI, or 1166.

Solution
1105

Explanation
5500 = VMVC
So the Roman numerals that make it up are
M, C, V
which makes MCV, or 1105.

Solution
66

Explanation
44= XLIV
So the Roman numerals that make it up are
L, X, V, I
which is to say, 66.

Medieval enigmas

Elixir
The vial cost half a crown. And not 1 crown, as one might imagine without thinking too much about it.

Explanation
If E is the value of the elixir and F the value of the vial, we have:

E + F = 30 and E = F + 29

If we replace E with its value in the first equation, we have:

F + 29 + F = 30

And thus 2F = 1, or F = 1/2 crown.

Smooth operator
The lute.

PAGE 9

The Big Barter
Jehanne has to go to stall 3 and exchange one of her pumpkins for a marrow. Then she should go to stall 2 and exchange the second pumpkin for two quails, then to stall 4, where she can exchange them for a bunch of leeks. Hurrah! She can go to stall 1 and get back a dozen delicious eggs!

PAGE 73

What am I?
A signature.

PAGE 20

Sunday's child
Because there are seven days in a week, there is one chance in seven that the young lady was born on a Sunday. All the other numbers have nothing to do with the probability of being born on one day or another.

The Damsel of the Short Sleeves
Taking advantage of the fact that the king is seated, the Ugly Damsel sits on his knees.

Merry-go-round
Arthur will have a bay horse.

Perceval will have a chestnut horse (which he appreciates, along with Lancelot, without however sharing the same feelings for the buckskin).

Lancelot will have the buckskin horse (the remaining knights don't want it).

And since Galahad doesn't like a dappled coat, he will receive the piebald horse.

Gawain will have no objections to being assigned the dappled horse.

The game of chess

The chronicle does not lie: they did indeed play chess, but against other adversaries.

There was nothing that obliged you to think that they played against each other.

The flush

The Queen will get back her comb in four days.

On the first day, the first pipe will have contributed to draining an eighth of the moat, the second pipe a twelfth and the third pipe a twenty-fourth.

$1/8 + 1/12 + 1/24 = 3/24 + 2/24 + 1/24 = 6/24 = 1/4$ of the moat in one day.

Four times more time is therefore needed to drain the whole moat.

One for three, three for eight

One of the knights cuts the loaf into two halves.
The next one places the two halves on top of each other and cuts down the middle again, to obtain four pieces.

The third one places the four pieces on top of each other, and with one strike of his sword obtains eight equal parts.

Oh how many unicorns, how many melusines …

3 Unicorns, 6 Pirassoipis, 5 serpents.
28 eyes makes 14 monsters
36 feet makes 9 quadrupeds, leaving the 5 Melusines who have a serpent body.

Let U be the Unicorns and P the Pirassoipis.
We know that U + P = 9
but also, counting by horns, that U + 2P = 15
therefore P = 6
and all that's left is 9 − 6 = 3 Unicorns

Thanking the squire

If the watchman saw the Lady of the Lake in a dream, he must have been sleeping; and if he was sleeping, he can't have been doing the job for which he is paid, which is to keep watch.

At home or on the town?

In the cemetery.

If the vavasour is a widower, it's because she's dead.

Featherweight

Since the birds have to be fed according to their respective weights, the budgerigar receives 21 ounces of millet, the jay 9 ounces and the third bird 15.

If we call the birds x, y and z, we can posit these three equations:

a) $x + y + z = 45$

b) $x = \frac{1}{4}(y + z)$

c) $z = x + y - 3$, hence $y = z - x + 3$

we can then reformulate the first equation a) as:

x + z — x + 3 + z = 45
2z = 42
z = 21

thus, according to a), x + y = 45 — 21 = 24
which we can reformulate using b) as:
¼ (y + z) + y = 24
y + z + 4y = 96
5y = 96 — z = 96 — 21 = 75
y = 15
thus x = 45 — (21 + 15) = 9
The budgerigar weighs 21 ounces, the jay weighs 9, and the third bird 15.

The Aymon boy nags

The eldest of the four Aymon boys is 9 years old.
Let H be the number of horses, which corresponds to the sum of the ages of the four brothers.

Five years before, each of the brothers was five years younger, so there were 5 x 4 = 20 fewer horses.

We can thus say:
H — 20 = C: 3 (since there were 3 times less than today)

$3H = H + 60$
$H = 30$

Five years before, the total of the respective ages of the sons was thus $30 - 20 = 10$ years.

But if they are all a different age, the only possibility for reaching a total of 10 is to add together $1+2+3+4$. Richardet, five years before, was thus one year old and the oldest four years old.

We just need to add 5 to find the current age of each of the Aymon boys: the youngest is six and the oldest nine.

PAGE 25

Just a question of time

If Mordred kills his grandfather before he was able to beget his father, he himself could not have been born, and he doesn't exist.

PAGE 120

Question for a champion

The knight will leave with the first cup: because in that case there

will indeed be just one true statement (the third) and three false ones.

On the other hand, if he chooses the silver cup, he is not paying attention to the fact that not only is the second inscription true, but also the first: it's one too many.

If he chooses the iron cup, only the second inscription would be false: he needs two more.

And if he chooses the golden cup, that implies that the first and third inscriptions are true.

The perilous bridge

Regardless of colour, the only solution is to ask one of the knights: 'If I ask the other knight whether the bridge he is guarding will allow me to cross the abyss, what answer will he give me?'

If your interlocutor says that the other knight will answer 'no', then the bridge in question is the one you must choose ...

It's simple logic: the knight who tells the truth can only give you the answer that the liar would give; and the one who lies will obviously give the opposite of the true answer. In both cases, if it's really the right bridge, the answer is 'no'!

Conversely, if your interlocutor tells you 'yes', rush without hesitating towards the bridge he himself is guarding.

The map is not the territory

Gawain opens the door and places the parchment on the floor so that the door closes precisely over the line that represents the waterway: half of it therefore is in the room the giant is in, and half outside, with the obstacle of the closed door in between.

Baring the teeth

Lancelot asks the dwarf to place on the scales one tooth from the first bag, two teeth from the second bag, three teeth from the third bag, and so on and so forth up to the eighth and last bag, then to perform the one and only weighing as promised.
If there were only cocodrile teeth, weighing 10 grains per tooth, the dwarf would get a weight of 360 grains (10+20+30+40+50+60+70+80).

If he gets 370 grains, then it must be that the tooth he took from the first bag weighed not 10 grains, but 20 grains: those ones are therefore the dragon teeth.

If it's 380, he should choose the second bag. If it's 390, the third. If it's 400, the fourth ... and so on.

Knight in green sauce

Everything of a knight that is edible will have disappeared in eight hours. In a full day, the lion can theoretically eat two knights, the wolf a third of a knight, the vultures a quarter and the maggots a twelfth.

$2/1 + 2/3 + 1/4 + 1/12$

$= 24/12 + 8/12 + 3/12 + 1/12$

$= 36/12$

$= 3/1$

If, through their combined forces and mandibles, the animals can devour three knights in a day, they'll need 1/3 of 24 hours to polish off the Green Knight, or 8 hours.

The accursed number

Perhaps you need to be a bit superstitious to recall that in Lancelot's time, Arabic numerals weren't yet in use in the

kingdom of Logres, and that the number seventeen was written
not as 17 but as XVII. However, XVII can be read as an anagram of
VIXI, which makes a Latin word meaning 'I have lived', which is to
say, 'I am dead' …

Even today, most Italian hotels don't have rooms numbered 17,
and in aeroplane seating seat no 16 is immediately followed by
no 18 … whether it is written, for that matter, in Roman numerals
or Arabic numerals!

PAGE 37

Apocalypse now

An army of 168 men.

x (the number of men) = 1/5x + 1/8x + 1/12x + 1/4x + 1/20x + 1/7x +
220 + 12 + 3 + 15

x = 715x/840 + 250

x = 715x/840 + 21000/840

840 x — 715x = 21000

125x = 21000

x = 21000: 125 = 168

Knights in search of a title

The red knight is a baron.

— One of the ladies lives in the same castle as the black knight (5), the castle of the king of Orkney (1), and as this lady knows how to play chess (5), it's not the duchess (3). Nor is it the countess, since she lives in another castle (1). It's thus the baroness who lives in the kingdom of Orkney.

— The lady who bears the same title as the black knight and who resides at Camelot (4) is thus not the baroness; nor is it the countess (1). It's thus the duchess, and consequently the duke is the black knight.

— The green knight, according to (6), cannot be a baron. We have just deduced that he can't be duke either: the title of count is all that's left. If the green knight is count and the black knight is duke, there's only room left for a red baron.

The legacy of the vavasour

Lancelot gets down from his horse and adds it to the stable horses. The division can thus be performed without a massacre:

Bors takes half of 18, or 9 horses; Galahad takes a third, or 6; and Perceval, who only receives a third, can put his longsword away and leave with 2 horses.

9 + 6 + 2 = 17: once the division has been carried out, and carried out properly, Lancelot takes back his horse. And can henceforth sleep soundly.

PAGE 44

Up to here

All you have to do is fill the container that holds a demiard and pour its contents into the chopine, which is to say, 300 millilitres into a container that holds 500 millilitres. Then you repeat this operation, taking care to stop at the precise moment the chopine is full to the brim: there will then remain in the first container the equivalent of a posson, which is to say exactly the 100 millilitres the cook asked for.

PAGE 50

At Wastefoolnesse Castle

At Wastefoolnesse Castle, it is obviously advisable to burn the candle at both ends. Brother Gastule counts an hour by allowing

a first candle to be completely consumed, then he lights two more at the same time, but he takes one of them out of the candelabra, puts it back onto the spike in the middle horizontally and lights it at both ends.

When it has completely burned down, he knows that half an hour has passed. Without extinguishing the other candle, he just needs to spike it horizontally in turn and light the wick at the other end: when the two flames meet, a quarter of an hour will have passed.

PAGE 51

The guillotine doors

The first ring must be turned 2 times, 1 turn for the second, 3 turns for the third and 7 for the fourth: the combination is 2137.

PAGE 53

No Bénédictine in the goblette

Bors first takes the goblin across; the dragon stays on the other side with the barrel, so there's no danger. Then he takes the barrel, but he can't leave them together, because the alcoholic goblin will help herself … so on the return trip he takes the goblin with him, whom he leaves on the riverbank while he takes the dragon across. He can then easily move away from the dragon and the barrel, and

169

go back to fetch the goblin. Another solution would be to take the dragon across after taking the goblin. The trick remains the same: the goblin has to be taken back to get the barrel across.

The Bridge of Mists

They have 28 minutes left, which theoretically is enough. Lancelot and Bors will cross the Bridge of Mists first: 4 minutes. Lancelot returns to the other side to give the necklace to the two other knights: 3 minutes. Perceval and Gawain cross over: 12 minutes.

At that point, 19 minutes have already elapsed, it's still raining and the suspense is about as much as the average solver of enigmas can take. Bors takes the necklace and will go to fetch Lancelot: 4 minutes more, making 23 minutes and in 5 minutes the grand massacre will commence.

With the sound of the spluttering of the giant-pile-of-mud Zieu audible amongst the howls of the wind and rustling of the pines, Bors and Lancelot dash out for the second time onto the Bridge of Mists and 4 minutes afterwards they are on the other side.

When the giant arrives, straining and coughing up his lungs, the bridge has no longer been standing for a whole minute, having once again evaporated into the mists, and the weather is still rainy.

I is for isosceles

The missing word is 'six': the whole sentence then contains six 'i's. (It should be noted that to assume that the missing word is 'five' is to forget that this word contains an 'i').

It is written

Bread (that must be obtained by the sweat of one's brow, as per the biblical maxim).

Bad at maths

Write down along one line the Roman numerals for the numbers ten, twelve and thirteen respectively: X, XII and XIII. Now draw a horizontal line passing exactly through the intersection of the Xs. The top half reads in order: V, VII and VIII, or five, seven and eight … You just passed your 'mad maths' exam.

Dragon steak

She starts by turning over the two hourglasses. When the sand in
the smallest one has run out, at the end of 13 minutes, she puts the
steak on to cook: during the time it takes for the sand in the larger
hourglass to run out, it cooks for 8 minutes.
As soon as it's finished, she just has to turn the same hourglass
back over to add 21 minutes, and Iseult the Fair has the desired
cooking time of 29 minutes.

Deluxe mustard pot

As soon as you have poured in one drop, the hanap is no longer
empty. As a result the answer, strictly logically, is one drop.

The solo crossing of the worm

The worm has completed a solo crossing of 45 centimetres.
Take a book and place it on a bookshelf, upright, with the spine
facing towards you: the first page isn't on the left side of the
book, but on the right side of the book in question. Which means

that the worm only crosses one of the wooden boards of the first volume. Similarly for the last volume, since he stops at the last page.

You thus add 0.5 cm + 0.5 cm for volumes 1 and 6, which gives you 1 cm, to which you need to add 4 × 11 cm for the four volumes in the middle (10 cm for the parchment pages and 1 cm for the board covers), or: 1 + 44 = 45 cm.

PAGE 71

The Fountain of the Three Maidens

Galahad turns the first ring, and waits 5 minutes. Then he turns it back the other way to return it to the off position, and activates the second ring.

He can then enter, observe and conclude: if the fountain is going, it's the second ring that made it work. If the water isn't flowing but the feet of the three statues are wet, it's the first ring that activated the mechanism and then interrupted it when Galahad put it back into its initial position.

And if the fountain is not going and the whole thing is completely dry, like an alabaster statue on which no water has flowed for the last two years, it's because the ring that operates the mechanism is the third ring.

The dragon can go cook himself an egg.

Small potatoes

Since at the last hand Gawain isn't holding a multiple of 2, he is the one who has lost. As a result, before this fifth hand, Bors had half as many as he has afterwards, namely 4 small potatoes, the same thing for Perceval, namely 5 small potatoes, and Gawain — who has just paid the two others — had 4 + 5 + 9 = 18 small potatoes. The loser of the previous hand was thus Perceval (the one with an odd number of small potatoes), and we can apply the same reasoning in order to understand the respective holdings of the players before this fourth round: 2 for Bors, 9 for Gawain, and 16 for Perceval.

In the third hand the loser could only be Gawain, which gives, at the end of the second round, holdings of 1 for Bors, 18 for Gawain, and 8 for Perceval. In the second hand, the loser being Bors, and the first round thus finished with holdings of 14 for Bors, 9 for Gawain and 4 for Perceval. Gawain being the loser of the first round, we can deduce from this that when they started, Bors had 7 clopinettes, Gawain has 18, and Perceval indeed only had two.

Massacres and making love

He learns two pieces of news at the same time: that his son is two years old, and that therefore this child cannot be his biologically. Michaud du Potaige was cuckolded.

If we represent the age of the child as x and the age of du Potaige as y, since we know that the child is 32 years younger than Du Potaige, we can say:

$x = y - 32$

As per the jester's second statement, when Du Potaige is six years older $(y + 6)$, the child, who will also be $x + 6$, will be 5 times younger, therefore:

$y + 6 = 5 (x + 6)$

$y + 6 = 5x + 30$

$y = 5x + 24$

We can now calculate the first equation using the value of what we have just worked out for y:

$x = 5x + 24 - 32$

$-8 = -4x$

$x = 2$

While the butcher of the Saracens butchered, his wife indulged

in fleshly pursuits of a rather less bloody kind: we won't go so far as to say fair's fair, but we won't be shedding any tears either. Especially since while he's a cuckold, he's a happy one: he now has an heir.

PAGE 79

Twelve feet minus the toes

Brother Gastule begins by placing a plank across one of the four corners formed by the moat around the square; the second plank is thus long enough to form a bridge between the point of the right angle of the yard opposite and the middle of this first plank. After you, my lord.

PAGE 80

Knife edge

Take the second of the vertical daggers and put it down horizontally so that it forms a line from the right-hand edge of the V above the dagger than forms the first I.
You have produced the sign that comes to us from the outline of the letter 'r', the first letter of 'Ramona, I had a wonderful dream' and of 'repeat that for me, please', but also of the Latin word 'radix', which means 'root', and the equation reads 'the square root of $1 = 1$': now it's a pure mathematical truth

Maniac!

And to finish off he puts his sword back in its sheath, because we said that he only acts between each stroke of the clock, and between 12 strokes there are only eleven intervals.

Chivalry and handicaps

No.
We know from (4) that the wandering knights who stutter don't go on horseback,
but these wandering knights on foot, we are told by (1), don't collect mushrooms,
but according to (3), the knights who collect mushrooms are the wandering knights who carry a sword,
however we know from (5) that the wandering knights who carry a sword also wear armour,
and from (2) that the wandering knights who go backwards wear armour.
As a result a wandering knight who stutters doesn't go backwards.

At the Castle of Pesme-Aventure
How many goblins are left? None.

Money for bling
In 14 hours and 24 minutes, Arthur will have earned his dream bling.

The horses produce 450 crowns in total in 24 hours or 1440 minutes. The 270 crowns thus require a period of 270 × 1440 / 450 = 864 minutes = 14 hours and 24 minutes.

Breton-style
My mother.

He who has drunk will drink again

There is barely more than a third of mead, properly speaking, left in the bottle. The first evening, the alcoholic monk drank one-seventh of the mead and replaced it with water.

The bottle thus contains a mixture of 1/7 water and 6/7 mead.
The second evening there is 6/7 squared of mead properly
speaking left, or between 0.73 and 0.74 litre, etc.
At the end of 7 days, there is 6/7 to the power of 7 of mead in the
litre of liquid in the bottle, or 0.34 litre.

PAGE 95

Tormented souls

Just one person: Brother Gastule.
All of the others whose path he crosses are going the other way:
they're returning pilgrims.

PAGE 98

Wool over their eyes

That makes a total of five monks: one gormless monk in the middle
of the room plus four tired monks, one in each corner, and each of
these four monks having in front of him the three others plus the
one in the middle.

PAGE 104

Not the hair

Your tongue.

A race against the grain

Each of them has mounted the horse of the other one. If Bors arrives first, Galahad will thus have lost, and vice versa.

Bag of tricks

The damsel has a few tricks up her sleeve as well: once she has pulled out one of the pieces of paper, instead of untying and unrolling it to read it, she feigns clumsiness and drops it into the fire.

'Not to worry,' she says to the jealous husband, 'all we have to do is read the one that's left to know what was on the one I drew out, since it will be the opposite … If it says "I live", kill me'

Restrictions
A surname.

She'll be apples

There are 90 priestesses.

Since Lancelot has eaten one of the 397 apples, the priestesses (P) share 396 apples (a) between them in the following way:

5/6 of P take 5 a

1/6 of P — 3 take 1 a

3 P take 3 a

$$396 a = (5a \times 5P/6) + (1a \times (1P/6 - 3)) + 3a \times 3P$$
$$= 25P/6 + P/6 - 3 + 9$$

$$396a + 3a - 9a = 26/6P$$

$$26P = 390 \times 6 = 2340$$

$$P = 90$$

Shall we check?

1 sixth of 90 = 15 priestesses, minus 3 = 12 priestesses who take 1 apple = 12 apples

5 sixths of 90 = 75 priestesses who take 5 apples = 375 apples

375 + 12 = 387, to which we add the 9 apples (of the last 3 priestesses) which makes 396, plus the apple that Lancelot ate to end up with the 397 apples harvested.

The star

David. D is a Roman numeral representing 500, just as the V represents 5. After subduing the Moabites, David defeated Hadadezer, King of Zobah, captured a thousand of his chariots and had all the hamstrings of his draught horses cut. No, really.

One-upmanship

Take your pick: triplets, quadruplets, quintuplets …

Friendship and sausages

Lancelot is pouting because, according to this logical and perfectly equitable division, Perceval's sausages are going to slip right through his fingers. Since the 20 dozen oysters are divided up equally, each of the four knights eats 5 dozen oysters. By the same token Lancelot has no need to be compensated for anything at all, and he won't eat any sausages. On the other hand, Bors loses a dozen of the oysters he has paid for and Galahad four dozen: the first will thus get two sausages, and the second eight.

Marketing

He'll need to capture 150 wandering knights.

If 12 dragons consume 36 knights in 18 days, then 3 dragons consume 9 knights in 18 days, and by multiplying by 3 to get the number of females, 9 dragons eat 27 knights in 18 days.

In 2 days, 9 dragons thus consume 3 knights.

In 8 days (the time it takes to get 12 eggs), 9 dragons consume 12 knights. We thus find that to get 12 eggs, we need to give 12 knights to the females to eat.

As a result, since we need as many knights as we want to produce of eggs, for 150 eggs we need 150 knights in the dragon's bowl.

Variation on a theme

The Sphinx. In order to show her that only man walks on four legs at the beginning of his life before he becomes a biped, Œdipus amputates the Sphinx's two front legs, which loll stupidly on the table between the ouzo and the water carafe, and heads off, leaving her his white cane, which he doesn't really need since his daughter Antigone, a real barnacle, goes everywhere with him and helps him avoid all the people who clutter up the footpaths between Thebes and Athens, saying, 'Before carking it, use the cane as you see fit, and thanks again for everything.'

Published in 2010 by Murdoch Books Pty Limited

Murdoch Books Australia
Pier 8/9
23 Hickson Road
Millers Point NSW 2000
Phone: +61 (0) 2 8220 2000
Fax: +61 (0) 2 8220 2558
www.murdochbooks.com.au

Murdoch Books UK Limited
Erico House, 6th Floor
93—99 Upper Richmond Road
Putney, London SW15 2TG
Phone: +44 (0) 20 8785 5995
Fax: +44 (0) 20 8785 5985
www.murdochbooks.co.uk

Publisher: Kay Scarlett
Editor: Sophie Hamley
Designer: Camille Durand-Kriegel

National Library of Australia Cataloguing-in-Publication Data
Author: Ly Maguy, Masson Nicole, Caudal Yann Martin Pierre
Title: Enigmas Celtic / Maguy Ly ... [et al.]
ISBN: 978-1-74196-820-0 (hbk.)
Series: Enigmas
Subjects: Puzzles--Medieval influences.
                   Games--Medieval influences.
                   Amusements--Medieval influences.
                   Psychological recreations--Medieval influences.
Other Authors/
Contributors: Ly, Maguy.
Dewey Number: 793.73

A catalogue record for this book is available from the British Library.

PRINTED IN CHINA.